Praise for Howard B. Schiffer's Work

How To Be A Family – The Operating Manual

"Written with tenderness, clarity, wit and sensitivity,
and full of sound common sense."

Sheila Kitzinger, author of The New Pregnancy & Childbirth,
The Complete Book of Pregnancy and Childbirth, and
The Experience of Childbirth

"Amid the growing number of superficial or tongue-in-cheek books about
what it means to raise children, this book shines like a diamond.
"Family" takes even the most casually interested reader on a journey into
the essence of creating family life. I would like every expectant parent to
be given this book. "How To Be A Family" contains the essence of what
'family values' is really about — holding your family
in the highest regard. Excellent."

Suzanne Arms, author of
Immaculate Deception and President of Birthing The Future

How To Be The Best Lover – A Guide For Teenage Boys

"This book will help young men and women all over the world learn what
it means to be a loving partner. Schiffer has broken ground for the
young men's movement, claiming the right for all men to be not just
sensitive, but transformative lovers."

Dr. Jennifer Freed, Co director of The Academy of Healing Arts for Teens

"Respectful, sensible, and heart-based, this is a unique and important book
for boys, and a gift to the women they will love in the future.
Parents of daughters should shout for joy!"

Jan Hunt, author of The Natural Child: Parenting from the Heart

HOW TO BE A FAMILY

THE OPERATING MANUAL

Also by Howard B. Schiffer:

How To Be The Best Lover -
A Guide for Teenage Boys

First Love / Remembrances

HOW TO BE A FAMILY

THE OPERATING MANUAL

Howard B. Schiffer

 Heartful Loving Press / Santa Barbara, CA
www.heartfullovingpress.com

The information contained in this book reflects the opinions, experiences and beliefs of the author. By checking with qualified authorities and professionals in this area, every effort has been made to assure that the information contained herein is accurate and complete. At the same time, neither the author or the publisher is engaged in giving professional advice or services to the individual reader. The ideas, information, and suggestions contained in this book are not intended as a substitute for consulting with qualified health care professionals, your family, and religious counselors. Neither the author or publisher shall be liable or responsible for any loss or damage allegedly arising from any information or suggestion in this book.

Heartful Loving Press
PO Box 30041
Santa Barbara, CA 93130

ISBN 0-9723639-1-2

Book designed by Jane Kutcher of 87 18 Creative Group

Library of Congress Control Number: 2003116846

Schiffer, Howard B.

How to be a family / The operating manual / Howard B. Schiffer

Includes index

ISBN 0-9723639-1-2

1. Parenting   2. Family Education   I. Title

For Stevenson

Dedicated to

Esther & Sam Schiffer

How to Be a Family:
The Operating Manual

ACKNOWLEDGEMENTS

My heartfelt love, admiration and appreciation to my own family; Kim, Austin, Zoë, Eliana and Kajetan. I could not do this without your support and love. It means everything.

To my dear wife Kim, you bring art and beauty into my life every day. Your continued commitment to growing and learning is always an inspiration.

Marthy Wellbaum, my dear friend and children's advocate par excellence. Thank you for reminding me about the first rule of parenting and for being such an extraordinary parent.

My brothers in the Santa Barbara Men's Community, you have shown me the power in men showing up (in all ways) for their families. You have reminded me of how nurturing men can be. To all who have revealed the beauty of men and helped me with this book, I thank you; Chris Mosio, Michael Friedman, Mark Daley, Mark Ruskin, Brad Fiedel, Alex Lobba, Michael Ryan and to all I have sat with.

Alex Lobba, my brother. For always being there one hundred per cent, I am eternally grateful.

Anna Bunting, sweet friend and always welcomed dinner guest, thanks for your genuine enthusiastic support.

Brad Fiedel, I appreciate your insights and dialogue on going through this process of creation. Thanks for showing up as a friend.

Rainbow, our dearly departed friend, for showing me how unique we all are, for always seeing the good in people, and for teaching us Dr. Valentino's trick of preferred restaurant seating.

Sandy Danaher, kind friend and dear soul, thank you for your complete support on how worthwhile this book is and for counseling with me through the process to get it done.

Elaine Lipson, dear friend and talented author of *The Organic Foods Sourcebook,* thank you for your generosity in helping with PR. Your support and enthusiasm are always appreciated.

Janice Cook Knight, your Friday morning laughter and smile are always welcomed. Thank you for seeing this as a book on heart-centered parenting, and the groundwork that makes everything else possible.

Ilene English, your vote of confidence in this work and nomination for us as model parents meant so much. Thank you for believing in this work.

Jane Kutcher of 8718 Creative Group, who again saw the unique heart of this work and turned it into art. Thank you for adding so much, I love working with you.

Priscilla Stuckey, your organization made this book make sense. I appreciate your outstanding talent as an editor and your genuine excitement about How To Be A Family.

Ezra Cooper, I never believed you could match the perfection of the cover you did for 'How To Be The Best Lover – A Guide For Teenage Boys', but you did it again with 'How To Be A Family'. Your art sees through to the essence of what I am trying to communicate. Your contribution is always the crowning touch.

And always to my family; aunt and uncles and cousins who have always been there for me, and to my extended family of dear friends who have shown me how you always get to decide how close you want to be with each other. I thank you all for the love.

THE GREAT DIVIDE

First you remember, as if in a dream or watching a piece of a thought float by. You get an idea, a vision of what it might be like. But you don't know. Something deep inside calls to you, but you question or don't pay attention to it. A part of you knows that your destiny lies here, and you are uncertain what to do with it.

Before I had kids there was a moment when I realized it could go either way. I had been in a few major relationships and was living alone, with a gorgeous house in a beautiful town, a business that was giving me a lot of money and freedom, a girlfriend, lots of close relationships, and even a number of wonderful kids in my life. I remember coming home one Saturday morning from my regular weekend bike ride. I had been up in the mountains, had stopped at the local café for some fresh juice and a muffin, and had biked all the way down to the beach. I came in and flopped down on the couch and knew I could stay there as long as I wanted.

At that moment the division was crystal clear. I was enjoying my life. I also had it pretty easy and knew that it would get a lot more challenging if I took on more responsibilities. Still, my life was satisfying. The decision to have a family would be huge and would change everything. I wasn't yearning. I had no empty feeling, like something was missing. Both options seemed fine. I was in my mid thirties, and it just seemed like something natural to consider. A possibility.

It wasn't until I turned forty that I got the message. The decades have always been markers for me. At twenty I retired, became a hippie, and started a commune in Oregon. At thirty I started my first business, which led to some success in the natural products industry. When I was forty I received the "family" message. It was very specific. I knew that if I did not have kids and a family, I would feel that I had missed something when I turned fifty.

Fortunately, right around that time I also met my wife, Kim, with the help of another clear message: "Marry this woman and you can have everything you want." Good information. Thank heaven I got out of my own way long enough to fall in love with and marry the woman I'm still crazy about. Our family now includes a son and two daughters. I am thankful every day.

Had I not made that decision fifteen years ago, all I would have now would be a clean house. Instead I have chaos and clutter and four other people I adore and get to share my life with. Pretty rich.

Parenting is the hardest thing I have ever done (by far) and also the best. In the most basic way it makes sense out of this life. Like love, it makes all the pieces fit together. It has been more work than I ever thought possible, and many days end with me putting my daughters down (my son is a teenager now) and falling asleep on their bed, completely exhausted and spent—nothing left. But like the Jackson Browne song says, "And when the morning light comes streamin' in, I'll get up and do it again. Amen."

With kids, the journey is an amazing one. Each step really is a new discovery. Along the way, I have picked up a few pieces of information. That's what this book is— the things that make a family work. It is the "operating manual" that should come with the first child. These are the things I have tried, tested against my own experience, and found to work. My suggestion to you is to do the same—try them on, see what fits, and put the rest in the recycling pile. Being a parent is an honorable thing to do with your life. I wish you the best on your journey.

Howard B. Schiffer

Santa Barbara, California

ADVOCATING FOR FAMILY

Everyone finds their own family. For some people, it is two people and a cat, or three dogs, and everything is fine. For others it is a group of close friends they can count on. This book focuses on one particular kind of family, the one with parents (or parent) and children (or child).

Different Families, Different Needs

Parent-child families also come in many different sizes and shapes. There are single-parent families (every single parent is a god or goddess—they should all have statues erected in their honor), the traditional two-parent families, extended families (where relatives or friends are actively involved in raising the kids), adoptive families, foster families, families with gay parents, stepfamilies, communal families, and just about any other arrangement you can think of.

Each type of family will face its own challenges. If you are in a stepparenting family, go to classes and participate in a group to learn about the special challenges you face. If you are a foster parent or gay parent or single parent, read about these special situations and meet and talk with other folks who have gone through these experiences before. Everyone has a little wisdom to share and can help you.

PART
ONE

MOVING FROM
ONE TO TWO

CHAPTER 1

FINDING THE RIGHT PARTNER

Finding the right partner isn't the icing on the cake, it is the cake. You can make a lot of improvements to your home—adding a swimming pool, putting on a new roof, doing a major remodel on the kitchen—but if the foundation is bad, you're on shaky ground. The right partner and your relationship form the foundation for your family.

Talk with anyone who is divorced and trying to raise their kids with a partner they're not aligned with, or to any single moms or dads who have been left as the sole parent, and you'll get an idea of how important choosing the right partner is. Make no mistake. You do get to choose. Your choice may be obscured at times by the heady giddiness of falling in love, a needing to heal from a painful relationship, or just a light relationship that continues past its expiration date. But whether it's by conscious decision or decision by default, the decision is yours, and it's one of the most important decisions you will ever make. This is especially true when children are involved. A partner who is aligned with you and in your corner through life's struggles will not make everything go right, but she or he will give you the support, reflection, and perspective to make it through the tough times and share the good times with as well.

For single parents the partner role can be filled by a consortium of supporters: a dear friend that you can pour your heart out to on the phone when you're at your wits' end; a support group of other single parents that knows what it's like having to get the lunches made, breakfast cooked, kids off to school, and childcare set up when you have an important business meeting to attend; a great baby-sitter who loves your child; honorary Aunties or Uncles who will take your child on special outings and show up for birthdays; relatives who will want your son or daughter to visit for spring break and will want every new photo; a doctor or health care provider you can trust; a neighbor to go for morning walks with; and maybe even a cooking club that delivers a hot meal to your home every Wednesday at 5:30 P.M.

However you set it up, you need a person or people you can trust and count on, so all of the other suggestions in this book can become possible. Finding them and knowing they are the right ones is a big decision.

The saving grace when I met my wife, Kim, was that we met on a plane and lived in different cities. One thousand three hundred and sixty-two miles between us made it a lot harder to be casual. Contemplating a move across the country, for either of us, carried a lot more weight in case it didn't work out. It made me get a lot more serious about what the relationship meant and what my commitment was.

Living in different time zones also gave me a lot more space to consider who this person was. It forced things to move slower and made our time together much more precious. It didn't allow that relaxed, extended dating situation where one thing leads to the next, and after six months you're living together without ever really confronting any major issues. Instead, our long-distance love focused the question, What are we doing together?

I've arrived at many life decisions almost by default, making them by virtue of not deciding to do anything else. In relationships this can lead to discomfort or dissatisfaction. One day you wake up and realize that you and your partner have very different sexual needs or are not lined up on the importance of material possessions. Yet even if this happens, there are only two of you to sort out.

When a child is involved, the complexity of these issues increases greatly. It is worthwhile, therefore, to consider some of these issues before you become two. So I offer you the list in the following chapter, which covers the key issues to consider in finding a partner—especially if you want kids or already have them. It is a list written in retrospect, after years of living with someone and seeing what works day in and day out. I know I couldn't have identified all these things beforehand, but if you haven't discussed them yet, you'll no doubt confront many of them in your first five years together. Save yourself time later, and go over these issues now, before they signal a gulf between you.

✤ *There are some decisions you make in life that affect your entire life, and who you have children with is one of them.*

CHAPTER 2

 ROAD CHECK

You are going on a journey, and your relationship is the vehicle you're going to be driving in. Your partner is the person you're going to be sharing the driving responsibilities with. You can still go on this journey if your car is a clunker and your partner doesn't drive, but it's going to be a lot more challenging. You may still get to your destination (raising your family), but it may be a very rough road. It's worth considering who you are going on this adventure with, and if your vehicle is in good enough shape to get you there. This list is the "road check" before you begin your trip.

Character—Does the person have a character you respect? Being trustworthy, kind, considerate, honest, ethical, and respectful is bottom-line for parenting. Deep respect for your partner will provide you juice when you think you're all out. Ask yourself, would this person be invited to sit at the Round Table?

Sense of Humor—Does the person like to laugh? Can she or he laugh at themselves? Or make you laugh? A sense of humor makes the difference between getting really upset that your teenager implied you were a fool and saying that thought out loud with a smile ("Dad, you're such a fool, don't you have any idea what I'm talking about?") so you can all laugh about it.

Chemistry—Is there a spark between you? It there electricity in the air when you are near? I am talking about not just sexual energy but also a deep attraction to the being of the other person. Your kids will notice everything—that you kiss and hug each other when you come home at night or that you sleep in separate beds. The chemistry is showing them that the relationship is current and alive and something they can count on.

Seeing the Best—Does the person bring out the best in you? Does she or he hold you in the highest regard? Or does this person nitpick and find fault with every little thing? Do you shine in the other's eyes? Look for someone who encourages you to reach higher and meet your goals. Their vision of you will set up how your kids see you as well. You can be the hero who can do everything or the bumbling incompetent who can't hammer a nail in.

Committed to Growth—Is this person committed to growing and learning? Does he or she read or go to classes or have some interest in becoming a better, more interesting, more alive person? It is impossible to figure out all life's challenges with kids beforehand, so it's a blessing to know your partner is actively searching for new and creative solutions to this week's obstacles.

Spiritual Path—Is the person on a spiritual path, and do your paths line up? Will you have to discuss which religion to raise the kids under? Think about Christmas, and if celebrating it will be a conflict. Consider how important is this to you or your relatives.

Values—Do you share the same values? The environment may be important to you or social issues, like doing service work, or recycling or politics or financial freedom. It's difficult for recycling or respecting the environment to be understood if your partner is leaving empty water bottles by the side of your trail on your hike. See if you line up in your respective needs for material possessions or for living in the country or the city. Where does each of you stand on monogamy? Consistent values create a safe framework through which kids can view the world.

Emotionally Mature—Is the person in touch with his or her feelings? Can this person express feelings and tell you what is going on, or are you always having to guess? You want someone who can express his or her feelings and at the same time be responsible for processing them in a non-disruptive way for your family. Is the person honest and available when you want to connect? If the answer now is "Not really," you can bet that under the added stress of children this person is sure to disappear. I once had a friend with three sons, and his wife always said there were four kids in the house. A partner who is playful can be a true joy, but one who is emotionally immature will just be one more kid for you to deal with.

Habits—Does this person drink? Smoke? Do drugs? As a pastime or as a career? Someone who has to medicate to go out into the world every day is not likely to be able to deal with the daily stresses of family life.

Lifetime Decisions—Do you both want to have a family, and if so, how large? See how closely you match when it comes to dividing up responsibilities and roles. Do you both want to have careers? How important is extended family to each of you?

Comfort Zone—Check the level of drama in your relationship. Are things basically comfortable with some occasional upsets, or are you fighting fires constantly? Do you enjoy just hanging out together? See what interests you share in your free time, like art, music, exercise, theater, sports, crossword puzzles, or reading. Do you really enjoy this person's company? This is the day-to-day stuff that makes life work.

Money and Financial Status—Is the person rich or dead broke? Has this person held a job in the last five years? Does either of you have career goals or financial aspirations? Do you have realistic plans on how to achieve your dreams? Money is one of the biggest stressors is relationships. Knowing you are both willing to work hard at jobs to achieve something can create a huge bond. Feeling like you're working overtime while your partner is hanging around with friends can lead to resentment and frustration. Again, kids are sensitive here; they want to feel secure that there will be food on the table every night, not anxious that the electricity got turned off again last week. This is not about being rich or poor, it's about having the basics covered and being in agreement about how to achieve that.

Rolling Up Your Sleeves—Are you both willing to work to make something happen? Can you go through hard times and learn and become closer through facing a challenge, or will you wilt and crumble? Watch to see if the other person chooses the easy way out or is willing to do the right thing, even if it is a stretch. Is this person strong in his or her inner core?

Career—Is this person a workaholic? Is there a balance in her or his life between home and work? What this will look like on a practical level is four out of five weeknights having dinner alone with the kids while your partner is working late at the office. Or all of the second-grade class plays that were missed because your mate couldn't get out of some business meetings. The message for kids here is that business comes first and they come after.

Friends—Does the person have some close friends? Who you hang out with says a lot about your character. Does this person's circle of friends support healthy habits and lifestyles? Will your relationship have room for outside friendships? See how each of you feels about the other remaining friends with a former lover or past spouse.

Partners—If an unexpected vacation came up, would you would be thrilled to get to spend two weeks alone with this person? Is the person your friend?

You Are Half of the Relationship

Of course, the other half of this equation is you. So after you think about the other person with all of the questions I raised, turn it around and ask the same questions of yourself. Do you have close friends? Healthy habits? Are you emotionally available? Do you like to laugh? And so on. A great practice if you're not in a relationship is to start working on these things now; then you'll know that at least half of any relationship you enter into will be healthy. It is also true that it is hard to find these qualities in another if you don't have them within yourself.

An Amazing Adventure, Day by Day

Relationships fix one thing—they give you someone to be with, someone to work with, someone to grow with, someone to talk to. It's a big thing but not everything. If your car was broken before your relationship, it will probably be broken after you find that someone special (unless you find a mechanic). Same with money—if you were poor before you fell in love, you will probably still be poor after you find Mr. or Ms. Right (unless they're loaded and generous). I used to say that it is all about waking up in the morning and seeing the other person before they have brushed their teeth or combed their hair and still being totally in love. At the beginning it is easy to throw caution to the wind and talk yourself into finding the quirky habit they have be somewhat interesting or amusing, especially if the sex is great. Cute weird habits wear thin over time. At some point it comes down to day-to-day life. That doesn't mean tedium and giving up the passion or the love. It means having someone there by your side who is willing to look at this as an amazing adventure that you are getting to do together.

PART

TWO

STARTING A FAMILY

CHAPTER 3

 DECIDING TO HAVE KIDS

Deciding to have children often isn't a decision at all. Sometimes you know there's "something we have to talk about" after you come home from a full day's work, but you just haven't gotten around to it. Or you bring your boyfriend or husband the piece of paper with the blue dot at the breakfast table. Or your wife or girlfriend gets surprised that she is feeling queasy in the morning.

DECIDING BEFORE YOU ARE PREGNANT

If you can start discussing the issues related to having kids before you are pregnant, you are better off. Having children is an enormous undertaking. It will change your life forever.

Parenting will force you to confront a million issues over the years. And if you are parenting with a partner, these issues will challenge you to come to a shared perspective. Do you want to have TV? What religion should the kids be raised in? Are you lenient or strict with discipline—being a noodle and letting the kids have everything or believing that 11:00 P.M. means you are home at 11:00 P.M. and not 11:15 P.M.? The list goes on and on.

So before you have kids, start thinking about these issues. If you have a partner, start talking about some of them and at least figure out where you are lined up and where you are not. If you do not have the luxury of discussing these things before you decide to have kids, you can do it while you are pregnant. You will definitely have to do it after your child is born. Decisions will have to be made, or your kids will make them for you. A few of the minor and major things to discuss:

The First Question

+ *Are you having children because you want to be loved or because you want to love?*

BB (BEFORE BIRTH) DECISIONS

Pregnancy can be an incredibly joyous time—to realize that your baby is growing and to begin to anticipate who that baby really is, what this new person will look like and thinking about how it might be to hold him or her in your arms. Pregnancy can also be filled with morning sickness, the daunting prospect of parenthood, and the fact that you can no longer see your toes when you look down. Either way, there are a number of issues that will come up rather quickly:

+ *Do you want to know the sex of your child?*

+ *How do you feel about amniocentesis—testing for possible genetic problems? Most babies are healthy, but you might want to discuss risk factors with your doctor if you have specific areas of concern.*

✤ Do both of you want to participate in the pregnancy—exercising, going to birth classes, being present at delivery?

✤ How much time can either or both of you take off after your child is born?

✤ Do you have family and friends to help you out with your new child?

✤ Whose last name will your child have? Obviously, you'll be picking first names as well.

✤ Which religion (if any) will your child be brought up in?

BABY'S HERE!

The issues that face you after the baby arrives start with the extremely immediate—cleaning up poop and pee and vomit—and end with large questions of lifestyle and community. Your perspective after your baby is here will be completely different. The specter of being woken up three times in the middle of the night shifts dramatically when you open your eyes and see your beautiful child beside you. There are also a million practical issues to consider, including:

✤ Who will wake up in the middle of the night to change a diaper or comfort a crying baby? You can switch nights or have shifts or have a designated person, depending on your schedules and responsibilities.

✤ Do you think cloth diapers are important, or are disposables okay? Do you want to have a diaper service? A diaper service is one of those great baby shower presents that you can appreciate for a long time.

✤ Will your child wear all-cotton fabrics, or are synthetics fine?

✤ Some folks want to pierce their baby's ears—it may even be an important cultural ritual—while other parents have a hard time even allowing a doctor to take a blood sample, so you may want to discuss this.

✤ Do your friends have children? Will you need to find a new group of folks to interact with (at least to find other children for your kids to play with)?

✤ Who will take care of birth control? How?

RAISING THE KID(S)

Childcare and child rearing are going to push most or all of your buttons. You'll need to decide how to arrange your parenting roles—completely shared, or one primary parent?—as well as how to schedule your time. Think you have a good idea of how much time parenting takes? Multiply this by ten! See yourself in the future: you're trying to get an important business letter done, and your seven-year-old interrupts you for the fourteenth time. It's a great opportunity to build those understanding, patience, kindness, and responsiveness muscles.

✤ Will one of you need to give up a career (or put it on hold) while your kids are young?

✤ Will you want to hire extra help with childcare?

✤ Who is cleaning house, making breakfast, handling social obligations like making plans to go out with friends?

✤ How much time does each of you need alone or for your work? Is there room to have a child?

✤ Are you willing to change your life around for your child in case of a special condition or illness?

✤ Do you feel you have had enough time by yourself to do things you wanted to do?

✤ Can you handle having a child on your hands when you are trying to rush around and get shopping and errands done?

SCHEDULING

Spontaneity gets tougher after a child is born. Scheduling starts with their eating and sleeping patterns. There's a rhythm, and you all have to make adjustments to meet each other's needs. The added challenge with babies, of course, is that their schedules change—they get sick or have a hard time sleeping or go through a developmental period, and everything shifts. The more you can get into a routine to meet your baby's needs and your own, the more resources you will have to be able to adapt when things change.

✤ Who will change their schedule around when your child gets sick and needs one of you to stay at home?

✤ Are you willing to rearrange your schedule to accommodate your child, like when they need to take a nap? There may be years when it is hard to do anything away from the house, like go to the beach, because a child needs to take a nap.

✤ Can you handle interruptions or things not getting finished because your kids need you to be with them? How about projects around the house taking three weeks to complete instead of a few hours?

HEALTH DECISIONS

Where your child's health is concerned, it is difficult to make a rational decision. Anyone who has ever had to sign a release form not to have their child receive a certain vaccination or had to hear a lecture from a parent or doctor on how irresponsible their decision was to not have a certain medical procedure done knows the trials you feel when you have to make a decision regarding your baby's health. In the moment it becomes almost impossible to weigh all of the pros and cons of any medical issue. Having some knowledge on the subject and talking to other parents who have faced similar decisions can leave you with some peace of mind when your time comes to decide.

* *Circumcision is an issue that people on both sides feel passionate about. Religious, cultural, health, and appearance are all considerations that come into play. Finding harmony between the two of you on this issue is of key importance.*

* *How about medical help—traditional or alternative, and in what situations? Think about whether you want to give your kids antibiotics or aspirin or homeopathics or some combination.*

* *How do you feel about vaccines?*

* *What do you want to feed your child? Do you think breast-feeding is important, or are you okay with formula? Think about whether you will want to make your own baby food when your child is ready or buy something off the shelf.*

FAMILY MATTERS

Once children are around, family takes on a new dimension, from that ring finger that is curved just like Grandpa's to the high cheekbones just like Aunt Sue to just a grimace in which you see your partner. You start to see how the currents run deep. You may also see that your parents, who may have advocated for not getting pregnant, or your siblings, who were emotionally distant, start to melt when they see your baby and acknowledge their new role as grandma or aunt. Kids love seeing where they came from and who else they are connected to in this life, so family for them is confirmation that they are part of something greater in this world.

✤ *If you are single, do you have extended family you will want to involve in raising your child? How close do you want your child to be to grandparents or cousins?*

✤ *If you are partnered, is it important that both of your families get to know your children? Think about how committed both of you are to making this happen, even if it would mean moving.*

AND A FEW OTHER MAJOR ISSUES

✤ *How do you feel about discipline and boundaries? Are you a pushover or very strict? For example, when your kid throws a tantrum in a restaurant, is that okay with you? Think about what you will do if your child is rude to a relative.*

✤ *Do you want your child educated in public schools, private schools or homeschooled?*

✤ *How do you feel about television for your child? Is Sesame Street a great way to start the day?*

✤ *Think about how you deal with children's emotions. Are you willing to let kids express feelings? Do you expect them to "snap out of it quickly," or are you into distracting them away from their feelings?*

WHERE YOU DO AND DON'T ALIGN WITH YOUR PARTNER

If you are partnered, you can see that many of these things will be non-issues for you both, while others will need a lot more thought. Obviously, you won't agree on everything. At the same time, if you are on opposite sides of the fence with some of the big ones, you may need to stop and see if you can arrive at a common ground.

If your mate says the child has to be raised Catholic and the whole family must go to church every Sunday, and this clashes with your being a practicing Buddhist, you probably need to talk. Likewise, if you are adamant about getting your son circumcised and your mate considers it infant mutilation, you need to see if you can reach a compromise. Hopefully you can both find the room to listen to what each other feels is important and find the flexibility to bend when you need to reach a middle ground.

CHAPTER 4

RESPONSIBILITY

My children's kindergarten teacher used to say that her only job was to provide a safe haven for the children and let them know they were welcome there and that their needs would be cared for. It is the same with being a parent—our job is to welcome the baby and say, "We're glad you are here; you are safe, and we will protect you." Big job. When a baby looks at you in complete innocence and you know that this little being is depending on you for everything, the totality of your commitment kicks in. It is a wonderful feeling and an awesome sense of responsibility.

FIGURE IT OUT FOR THEM TOO?

Many of us are still trying to "figure it out" or learn what our own destiny is in this world. We may wonder, how can we figure it for our kids too?

The secret is, you don't have to. In fact, it is probably unrealistic or delusional to think that you would or even could. You're changing, they're changing, and the world is changing too rapidly.

♣ *Another big secret—you're going to blow it sometimes.*

What you can do is show up for them and be your best. You can adopt a way of seeing the world and your kids that will allow you to adapt and deal with what's in front of you on any given day.

THEY JUST WANT YOU

The amazing thing is that kids are willing to believe in you (until they become teenagers at least), so you already have a fan club rooting for you to succeed. You don't have to have your financial future sealed up. Kids are pretty flexible and resilient, especially when they are younger. They just want you.

A friend of mine who usually spends long hours at work was going to do childcare one weekend while his wife went away. He started planning all the activities he would need to keep them busy—movies, a trip to the beach, going to the local playground, eating out, and so on. Then he hurt himself going down the stairs first thing Saturday morning. Instantly he panicked, watching all his plans go up in smoke. An hour later his kids awoke, came downstairs, and jumped all over him while he was sitting on the floor. They didn't leave for several hours, and at that point he got it: they were delighted. They just wanted to be with him, and everything else was a distraction. It was a revelation—and he could have missed it by being too busy or trying too hard. Slowing down gave him just enough time to see what his kids needed.

SHOWING UP FOR THE SMALL THINGS

With kids, a lot of the responsibility is just showing up for the small things.

Being there to pick them up from school. Playing a card game with them even though you are busy and need to get some work done before dinner. Staying up with them and comforting them when they get sick. Noticing when they are going through a difficult time and being available to talk about it. Seeing what is important to them so that when their birthday rolls around you can get a present that means something. Putting their photograph on your desk at work. Or really appreciating a drawing they made for you or a figure they put together out of beeswax or wood and fabric.

All of these things mean you are noticing them. You are acknowledging in word and action that they are there and they are important in your life. For kids to build self-esteem, this is one of the most important ingredients (in psychology it's called "mirroring").

❖ *Having a parent see kids for who they are and acknowledge how special they are goes a long way toward building kids' sense of self-worth.*

LOVE THEM

The other major responsibility, of course, is love. You need to show and tell your children regularly how much you adore them. Kids have great bull detectors, so if you give lip service to love but don't come through for them by showing up at their school play or being there when they really need you, they will learn not to expect much.

The hard thing about parenting is that it goes on day in and day out, and the responsibility continues for at least eighteen years (and in truth for much longer).

What you are saying to your kids when you sign up for this is that you will try your best to hold it together for them—financially, with a home for them to grow up in; in your relationship with your mate, if you have one; and in providing food for them. It's the "I will keep the basics covered" pledge. You don't have to be rich to do this. Plenty of kids grow up without wealth, but they see their parents showing up and working to make a life for them, and that means the world to them.

A dad whose son was on the all-star basketball team my son was on would sweep the floors and clean up the gym before and after every practice so his kid could play. This dad couldn't afford the coaching fees or the entrance costs for tournament play, but he paid for it by doing a work exchange. Today this kid is a great ballplayer. I know a lot of his motivation comes from seeing how much his dad did to make it possible for him to play.

A filmmaker awhile back at our local film festival had done a project on the people in his neighborhood. These were just regular folks going to work, fixing their cars, and talking about how they were going to pay their bills. At the end of the film, he said, "You know, these people are my heroes. They are the people who just wake up and go to work every day and try to keep it together for their family." That is it—taking the responsibility and embracing it. It is a heroic gesture and a truly noble thing to do.

CHAPTER 5

BONDING

Holding your baby for the first time is a moment in your life that you never forget. It is one of those rare times when your heart bursts completely open. You are connected to the miracle of life in the most profound and basic way. Hopefully this moment is a start, and your heart will open to your child many times as she or he is growing up. Parents who meet their children later in the kids' lives through adoption or stepparenting wait to find these times. Moments when your heart bursts open are part of the bonding experience and an essential part of building a family.

THE BOND IS CELLULAR

Years ago I worked as a midwife in California (a whole story in itself), and one of my colleagues, Raven Lang, who wrote The Birth Book (Genesis Press, 1972 — out of print), was a pioneer in the home birth movement. She was one of the first to identify (and write a groundbreaking paper on) the bonding experience.

Raven gave birth to her child at the local community hospital and recuperated in the ward with about twenty other new moms. At this time moms and babies didn't get to stay with each other the whole time (which thankfully has changed in most hospitals now—a result, I believe, of Raven's work). Every day the nurses would bring the babies in one by one at specific times for nursing and feeding. Usually the babies appeared in alphabetical order, and since Raven's last name was in the middle of the alphabet, about fifteen minutes would pass before she would get to see and feed her baby. One day nursing time came, and the third baby brought into the ward started to cry, and Raven's entire body reacted. Her uterus contracted, her breasts started aching, and she knew it was her baby. The nurses had decided to switch the order that day and had started with the end of the alphabet. Raven's physical response prompted her research into how important the bonding is that occurs between mothers and babies. We now know that the bonding in fact occurs with the entire family, which is why it is so important to keep the family together during the first part of the baby's life.

THE GLUE THAT STICKS

Bonding is the glue that can hold a family together. Moms can feel it as a physical sensation—that this being who once grew inside them is still connected body and soul in a very tangible way. Dads can feel the bonding in their bodies as well, from their body clenching with a protective instinct when their kids might be in danger, to their bad mood melting away when their child's face lights up upon seeing them.

As the child grows up, the bonding remains a point of reference, something to go back to that helps you remember your connection as a family. This bonding occurs naturally from just spending time together, playing with each other, sharing the many firsts that your baby goes through—from rolling over to holding their head up to imitating you to crawling and gurgling first words. For moms the bonding is organic, since the baby associates the mother's smell, sound, and touch with its very nourishment. Moms who are there for their kids and accept this responsibility can feel this bond almost at a cellular level. For dads and siblings, this bonding sometimes takes a little more intention, although it can be quite powerful as well. This is true for adoptive families and stepfamilies too—bonding is a possibility but you may just have to put more effort into developing it, depending on the age of your child. Every time you stop to listen to your baby breathing, wake up with her in the middle of the night to comfort her, get him into bed with you when he's scared, or have her fall asleep in your arms at the end of a long day, and during a million other moments of heart-to-heart connection, the bond is built.

The bonding goes beyond words. It is the place you return to when your rational mind stops and you feel, at the very core of your being, how open your heart is and how deeply connected you are to this other person.

SETTING THE STAGE FOR BONDING

In the first few weeks of a baby's life, you have a prime opportunity to bond with your child and to bond together as a family. It just takes time and attention and not too many distractions. For this reason it is great to have a "food tree" set up after the birth of your child, with friends and family dropping by food at prescribed times (and hopefully not staying too long, or at all) so you can have your basic needs met. Then you can just revel in the mystery of getting to know a new soul in your life. It is a magical time. For parents who get to know their children later in the kids' lives, this bonding is still essential, and it is important to set aside time for it.

When my son started living with me he was three, and I tell people that for the first two years after he and his mom and I became a family, I ended up spending more time with him than with my wife. That's how long it took. I really needed to show up and let him know that I would be there for him.

Adoptive parents talk about "claiming," whereby you decide that you are going to be there for that child even before you have an emotional relationship and definitely before you have bonded. It's a conscious decision you make. That is what I did with my son, and it was the commitment that allowed the bonding to happen.

For adults who never had anyone show up for them as children, this can be a particular challenge. If no one chose to make you a priority, you may have to make a concerted effort to learn and practice this skill. As with many things in parenting, it sometimes is a learned behavior. That's the good news. You don't have to be a natural in the parenting role to be a great mom or dad. Many of the best moms and dads I know grew up in awful situations, with parents who were alcoholics or abused them. As adults they committed themselves to changing the pattern with their own kids, and after a lot of work, they are some of the best parents I know. You have an opportunity to break the chain of neglect and absentee parenting.

MAKE THIS TIME A PRIORITY!

Whatever else you do, set aside this time to be with your baby. This might mean taking the first few weeks off from work after your child is born (or after you adopt or are first a stepfamily) just to settle in together. Kids grow up so quickly, and the amount of things that happen in these first two years is monumental. When they are really young they also have an openness that changes as they get older. Infants and toddlers are totally dependent on you, and consequently they are completely trusting in you. Their love is unqualified and complete.

When my younger daughter, Eliana, was a few weeks old, and we had been together almost every minute since her birth, I had to leave on an errand one day. I went to kiss her good-bye, and she just burst into tears—big uncontrollable sobs. Being separated was huge for her, and my heart just crunched when I felt that. I needed to let her know that this was coming and that it would only be a short while until I returned. Just stopping and telling her where I was going would have gone a long way toward comforting her and easing her distress. On one level babies are totally helpless, and at the same time they are completely present and paying attention to everything that goes on around them. They may not understand your words, but they can clearly understand your intention.

TRACTOR BEAM ATTENTION

When she was only a few months old, Eliana was sitting in a carrier on the floor in our home, just amusing herself as family life went on around her. A friend, Marilyn, came over, and I noticed Eliana following her every move as Marilyn said hi to everyone—except the baby on the floor. Our friend then sat down at the table and started talking to us. The conversation went on for a while, and then Marilyn suddenly looked over at Ellie, who started smiling and cooing when she saw Marilyn noticing her. Later Marilyn told us that she just "felt" someone's attention on her when she was sitting at the table, and suddenly she realized that Eliana had her in her beam. Ellie just wanted to say hello and be recognized. Kind of simple.

Time Slows Down

When babies are young big changes come fast, and time seems to move slowly. When they are two days old, one day is half of their life. Then a week is half their life, then a month, and so on. Your experience with them changes accordingly, so that time appears to speed up as they get older. It seems to take them such a long time to walk, and then suddenly they are running. Then you see a photograph one day and you realize this is not a baby anymore but a toddler. It's a great reminder to pay attention.

In the movie Hook, the grown-up Peter Pan has forgotten his past and is a corporate executive, rushing around in his busy life. His wife, who is trying to slow him down, says, "We have a few special years with our children...it's so fast Peter...it's a few years and then it's over..." It's true. I remember when Austin was seven and really wanted to be with me, I decided to spend one "special" hour on an outing with him every week. My work life was busy at that time, and somehow two years went by before I realized that I had totally blown my promise to him.

Real life happens, not at the big events like birthdays and holidays, but in making peanut butter and jelly sandwiches every day or putting Band-Aids™ on "owies" or cuddling in the morning or just watching them totally absorbed in their fantasy life. All you have to do is be there.

They're Fully Aware

Rule #1: Listen to your kids as fully aware people. They are.

Rule #2: Speak to your kids as fully aware people. They are.

New research by Dr. Ray F. Castellino from Birthing Evolution / Birth

Awareness (BEBA) is showing that newborn babies have a tremendous awareness of everything going on in their environment. Dr. Castellino has documented young children who without coaching or prompting could recreate their birth environment, accurately recalling who was in the room and where they stood, even down to the details of pinpointing a pair of surgical scissors on the table!

When my kids were still infants and preverbal, I always assumed they were fully cognizant and aware of their surroundings, and I treated them accordingly. Besides setting up a strong connection with your children this way, you are giving them the utmost respect, which is the basic building block for self-esteem and self-worth.

THREE

YOUR OWN LITTLE
UNIVERSE

CHAPTER 6

THE GROOVE

Here are two seemingly contradictory traits:

* *Kids are resilient and adaptable to change, and*
* *Kids love routines.*

The resiliency in children comes from the reality of their situation—you are calling the shots, and they have to conform to your decisions (or struggle with you). They are also more adaptable than most adults. If you have to move or go through a marital change, they really can't influence the outcome, they have to adapt. It's hard and they do it. On another level they may not be as attached to "things as they are" as most adults, so they have more room to be flexible.

The caveat here is that when change is thrust upon kids they may react in ways we don't expect or initially see. After friends of ours moved, their daughter began to show frustration in school by getting easily upset with her friends and not cooperating with her teacher. With the help of an astute teacher, her parents were able to see that this was her way of responding to the many changes in her life.

DON'T MOVE MY RICE MILK

Children love routines. Knowing what is going to happen makes the world safe for them. They know who is going to pick them up from school. They trust that someone is going to make breakfast for them in the morning. I remember that before Kim and I were even living together, when Austin was about two and a half, a lot of major changes took place in his life. During that time there were two things he loved: his bed—it was the constant amid a few moves—and his breakfast routine. One morning, I remember, I moved his fork and his rice milk to a different spot in front of him, and he just fell apart. I was rearranging his solar system. I quickly put things back in order.

STARTING THE DAY RIGHT

Breakfast is a great way to start the day. Food is important, not just as a nutritional source but also because it begins the daily ritual. Kids see you cooking, and the message they get is that they are important and you are nurturing them. How you cook and decide to have meals with your family says a lot about how you care for each other.

I believe in protein as providing a strong nutritional foundation for my kids before they go off to school. I also like to have things ready for them when they wake up. So I get up at 6:00 A.M. and give myself thirty to forty minutes before I start waking them up. I'll then fix everyone a hot breakfast of eggs and toast and have the cereal and milk out too.

Kids need a good start in the morning, whatever your dietary preferences.

Breakfast is also a great way to connect in the morning and to start the day as a family, even if no one is real chatty first thing in the day. My son, for example, who is now fifteen, is not a great conversationalist until he has had three eggs, two to three bowls of cereal, two big glasses of water, and some toast.

I also use the mornings to make sure everyone is covered for lunch. My wife and I switch off in the job of making their lunches, and when she takes the lead I assist and make sure they are balanced and complete. Our routine is a sandwich, piece of fruit, veggie (carrot or celery), and maybe a snack (chips or nuts). There also have been long periods when peanut butter and jelly sandwiches were the mainstay of our lunches, and that was the best I could do. The main thing is some basic nutrition, and consistency in making sure lunch is fixed.

With good lunches you may end up affecting other kids as well. If junk food is the rule at your school, your child may feel deprived or become very adept at trading. But if most kids are packing healthy lunches, carrot sticks and a juicy peach will become the norm.

Mornings didn't always work so well. We used to have major drama around our house getting the kids ready for school. Kim would be screaming because no one was ready, and the kids would be in tears by the time they got in the car. Not a great way to start the day. So we sat down as a family and talked about it. The kids were given the power to put up a hand and say, "Mom, it's not okay when you yell," I got involved with helping to make breakfast and lunches, and we all made more of an effort to get out the door on time. The results were completely worth it. Now everyone gets fed, lunches are made and complete, and we all leave the house in a good mood. A much better way to start the day.

POETRY IN THE MORNING

Morning verse is something we do in the car on the way to school. It helps us start the day connected to each other. All we do is say a poem together and talk about what each of us is grateful for. My wife started it with the kids, and then when I began taking them to school more often, I picked up on it, as it was such a great thing to do. The alternative would have been light conversation or silence.

Our morning verse is something Kim picked up from a book called *Seven Times the Sun: Guiding Your Child Through the Rhythms of the Day*, by Shea Darian (Gilead Press, 1999). The poem goes like this:

Open wide the door to morning,

Take love as you depart,

Walk gently on the earth,

With kindness in your heart.

Open wide the door to morning,

Take courage as you go,

Stand for the small and helpless,

Work for the good to grow.

Open wide the door to morning,

Take beauty as a clay,

And mold an act of thankfulness

For the blessing of this day.

After we all say the verse together, we go around and say what we are thankful for. Listening to what each person comes up with every morning is just incredible. For me, it's a great time to be honest with myself and my kids about what is important and what I am thankful for in my life. For them it's a great reminder when they hear me say that I am thankful for each of them and our health and how much we love each other. My teenage son might be thankful for music or food or living here or the fact that it's a gorgeous day or that he has a basketball game to play that night. My older daughter might be thankful for her friends, her grandparents, a song she is learning on piano, a book she is reading, or a games class she has at school that day. And my younger daughter is always thankful for her family and all the people who love us, for the fact that we live in a beautiful place, and recently for the little white bunny that is hopping around our neighborhood. It really is hard to be in a bad mood when you start your day like that.

If you start your kids early in their lives with a morning verse, they enjoy it as part of their routine. For parents who try introducing it later, you may get some rolled eyes and resistance. You can jump-start this by being committed to saying it every morning at a certain time and asking the kids to join in with you. If you are the first one saying what you are thankful for after the verse, speak from your heart and include real things from their lives in your gratitude. It will go a long way toward having them want to participate. There are also times when my children can only get out one or two things they are thankful for, or maybe just can't say anything that day, and I always give them room to be silent as well.

I know this ritual would never have happened in my family when I was a kid. Getting to school for me meant dodging kids who were beating each other up on the school bus. I can tell you that this is a lot nicer way to begin the day.

FEED ME!

After school, we try to get some nutritious food in our kids quickly, as they are usually starving. It is a good time to check in and see what homework they have or if there's any special news we need to hear about school activities.

TWO SOURCES OF NOURISHMENT

Dinner we always try to do together. We light candles at dinner every night, to change the atmosphere. We also try to clear the table and create a peaceful space in which to eat. Our rule is that we all show up for dinner. This may shift in the summer and on weekends, but most of the time we make it happen. It is extremely important for families, especially as everyone gets older and more involved with their lives, to have time to connect at least once a day, all together.

We always start the evening meal with a blessing. This is something I never did growing up, and I probably even had some attitude about it. But I have seen with my kids that it helps us all stop before we eat, slow down enough to be together, and have the chance to acknowledge how blessed we are to be able to be together and to eat good food. Our blessings vary.

We may sing songs, like our version of the Johnny Appleseed song:

Oh, the world is good to me,

And so I thank the world,

For giving me the things I need,

The sun and the rain and the appleseed,

Oh, the world is good to me.

We usually end with holding hands around the table and saying, "Blessings on our meal, our family, and our friends."

If friends are present, we take the time to thank them for being there with us.

Another poem we use is one the kids learned at school, and it has fun hand motions:

Earth who gives to us this food,

Sun that makes it ripe and good,

Dear earth, dear sun,

By you we live,

Our loving thanks to you we give.

One of the poems we sing as a song:

For the golden corn,

For the apples on the tree,

For the golden meadows,

And the honey for our tea,

For fruits and nuts and berries

That grow beside the way,

For birds and bees and flowers

We're thankful every day.

Another poem set to music that we love:

The silver rain, the shining sun,

And fields where scarlet poppies run,

And every ripple of the wheat

Is in the bread that we do eat.

So when we sit at every meal

And say our grace, we always feel

That we are eating rain and sun,

And fields where scarlet poppies run.

One of our Italian friends taught us the following blessing, which we love because it ends with "Ma, Ma, Muci," which we say with gusto. Our friend says there really is no translation for this ending, but it always makes us laugh:

Per questo pan (For this bread)

Per ogni ben (For all good things)

Noi ti lodiam, Signor (We praise you, Lord)

Ma, Ma, Muci

WHAT PHONE?

We also don't answer the phone during dinners. The truth is, we don't answer the phone much at all. It drives our friends crazy, but we have chosen to have a more serene home life than you can have when someone is jumping up to answer every phone call. We do have voice-mail, which fortunately holds twenty messages, although many times it is full because days go by with no one checking. But during dinner it is a hard-and-fast rule: don't answer the phone. It allows us to be together and not be distracted or interrupted.

I WISH YOU GOOD NIGHT

Bedtimes are so essential. I'll go into it later in "The Basics" section, but suffice to say, it is essential to your health to get a good night's sleep. Starting bedtime at a reasonable hour also gives you time to do an evening ritual with your kids. The ones that have worked great for us are:

+ *Telling stories*

+ *Reading books*

+ *Playing music*

+ *Singing*

Stories can be made up, based loosely on the kids' lives, with people they recognize going on adventures. Or you might tell your children stories about their past or their ancestry. The type of story doesn't matter, as long as it is from your heart. It is great if at times the stories are continuing, and you tell one piece or one adventure each evening. If you are a great storyteller, maybe you can do this every night. For me, the ongoing stories are a special event and are told maybe once or twice a month. The kids love them, and it is amazing how well they remember the details. At times I have been so tired that I start telling a story and end up falling asleep in the middle of the story, before the kids nod off. In the morning, they always tell me at what point in the story I fell asleep.

When my son was young and a very active guy, I told stories for years in which he and his friends would go off on long, exciting motorcycle rides. One of his friends, who loved to eat, would always be the comic relief, packing a ton of food and asking all the time when they were going to stop next to have a snack. My daughters' stories have centered on a mythical cat named Rafaella (based on a cat from my childhood). Rafaella stories are always the biggest treat for them. Girls also love adventure stories, especially ones where the main character is a girl so they can easily identify with the sense of excitement.

ARE YOU CRYING, DAD?

Research has shown that children who are read to turn out to be better readers. So reading stories to your children is also a great thing to do before bed. You can find many absolutely great children's books nowadays. Often they completely move me—my kids watch for tears to come during very emotional spots or will say to me, "Dad, you should read this one. It will definitely make you cry." They know me.

A bedtime reading routine also can tie in nicely with getting your children to the library—one of the greatest institutions in the civilized world. Visiting the library is a great ritual to do together. You can choose books together and separately and then read them as part of your bedtime routine. Chapter books are also wonderful as kids get into school. You get to have some continuity from night to night, and your kids get to use their imaginations to picture what is happening.

PLAY ME TO SLEEP

If you play piano or guitar or any soothing instrument, playing music for your children is a wonderful gift to give them at night. It also lets them transition into sleep with something to open their hearts at the same time. The fact that the music is coming from someone who loves them is a treasure they will always remember. Playing for them isn't the same as turning on a music box (which also can be nice sometimes) or using a tape or CD. There is something about your giving them the music that allows them to receive it in a qualitatively different way, at a much deeper level.

SURROUNDED BY LOVE

For anyone who doesn't play an instrument, the best instrument of all is your own voice. I could never sing or carry a note—I always had stuffed-up sinuses, and getting a tone was impossible. When my kids were small, though, I really wanted to be able to sing them to sleep at night. Because they were young and didn't know about being off-key, I thought I could give it a shot. It was more important for me to try than to let my embarrassment stop me. So I kept singing, and it got better. It was a miracle that I actually became able to carry a tune and give them songs that I loved at night.

The variety of songs we share is large. It ranges from folk songs, like Peter, Paul and Mary's "Autumn to May" or Richard Fariña and Pauline Marden's "Pack Up Your Sorrows," to Joni Mitchell's "Both Sides Now" or "Circle Game" or Carole King's "Child of Mine" or "What Would I Do?" I might sing "City of New Orleans" by Steve Goodman or "Dixie Chicken" or "Willin'," by Little Feat. It's an eclectic mix. I usually end with a version of "Lullaby," (Johannes Brahms, Eng. Anon.) for which I made up some additional words:

Lullaby and good night, in your dreams I will hold you,

Lullaby and good night, I will always be right here.

Lullaby and good night, I will love you forever,

Always and ever, every day of my life.

I love you, yes I do, and I want you to know,

Everywhere, anywhere, that you ever, ever go,

I'll be here, by your side, and I'll love you forever,

Always and ever, every day of my life.

Like I said, it often puts me to sleep too. Many nights I doze off in their beds, waking again at 10:30 or 11:00 P.M. and then dragging myself upstairs to my bed. It's a little disruptive to my night's sleep, but I so enjoy the time with my children in that dreamy state before sleep that it is worth it. Remember, you are opening the door to dreamland for them, so the stage you set and the feeling in the room allows them to end their day surrounded by your love.

CHAPTER 7

THE BASICS

Years ago, before I was a parent, someone I knew with three young kids told me, "There are only two things you need to make sure of with kids:

1. *Make sure they eat.*
2. *Make sure they sleep.*

The "only" is a gross oversimplification, and yet in retrospect I realize the wisdom in the words. Eating and sleeping are really the bottom line.

Having kids can teach you the basics of what the human body needs to survive and thrive: nutrition, sleep, and exercise. Kids are naturally active given a little room to move, so with most kids the third part of the equation will be handled. The other two, though—food and sleep—really need your help and support.

THE BROKEN-COOKIE SYNDROME

The first time you watch your child fall apart in the "Broken Cookie

Syndrome," you will go through all the confusion, frustration, and anger that many parents feel when they can't fix the problem. Your child, who moments before seemed to be having a great time, is suddenly in tears with no explanation. A cookie broke, or she is earnestly trying to ask you for something and you cannot figure out her words, or he bumped his toe and now it sounds like he just had his entire foot chopped off. So you get a new cookie, or you scramble through every word that sounds like "ball" but obviously isn't, or you try every remedy on the "owie," and nothing is comforting. You try holding her, cuddling him, allowing them time to express their emotions, and it just keeps going on. As you run out of tricks, you go from confusion to frustration, and finally some anger creeps in as nothing works and you begin to come up against your own exhaustion.

MOMENT OF BRILLIANT INSIGHT

Then a light goes on. It is the moment of brilliant insight. You realize that your child's response is simply out of proportion to what happened. You begin to remember your sweet child and to stop thinking that your baby was switched with the "evil" baby in the hospital. You stop saying, "I can't do this" or "I'm done." Hopefully, you have stopped yourself from screaming. Because you remember:

❖ *It is now 5:00 P.M. and your child has not eaten anything since lunch, and she has been playing hard all afternoon and she is hungry; or*

❖ *It is now 7:00 P.M. and your child did not get a nap this afternoon and he had a full day and is probably exhausted.*

I Hear You, Eat This

When our children were small and would get upset, we sometimes sat them down at the table and started feeding them, right in the middle of their tears and hysteria. We would sit beside them and continue listening to the upset, bobbing our heads up and down, saying "Uh-huh" over and over again, with attentive concern on our faces, the whole while making sure that food kept going in their mouths. And just as if we had spooned them a magic potion, their tears suddenly stopped, they calmed down, and our wonderful child was returned to us.

Short-Order Chefs

When we have a lot of kids staying over at our house on sleepovers or on the weekend, we usually feel like we are running a restaurant. We make sure the kids have a good breakfast (hopefully with some protein in it, to give them sustained energy), we make sure to have a snack out a couple of hours later (some fruit or cheese and crackers or peanut butter and apples), then it is time for lunch, and two or three hours later they need some afternoon snacks and then . . . you get the picture. We also make sure they are all drinking a lot of water so they stay hydrated.

So many problems and upsets and fights can be avoided if they are eating properly. Dr. Stephen Schoenthaler, who has done extensive research with kids and nutrition in juvenile halls, has shown that with proper nutrition, in a very short period of time, the incidents of noncooperation, verbal abuse, physical assaults, and poor attitude drop dramatically. Kids need to eat regularly and frequently, and the better their nutrition, the better their mood. Stay away from fast foods and chips and sugars (natural or refined). Go for organic, unprocessed food, as close to its original form as possible.

My mom was a third-grade teacher, and she would always say the worst day of the year was the day after Halloween. Lots of sugar and not a lot of sleep—the perfect combination for a guaranteed disaster.

Sweet Dreams

The other major component of a child's well-being is sleep. Children need sleep, and they need a lot of it. Your part of this process is twofold:

* *Set up a regular schedule for bedtime and then stick to it.*

* *Set up the environment in their room so they can sleep undisturbed and soundly.*

I am always amazed when we go downtown at night and see parents out with their kids on school nights at 10:00 P.M. I don't see how those kids are going to be in good shape the next morning. Dr. James Maas (Power Sleep: Preparing Your Mind for Peak Performance, published by Harper Collins), who is the world's leading educator on sleep, says that kids need a minimum of 8 or 9 hours of sleep every night. By the time they are teenagers, they need 9.25 hours every night. If your kids wake up early (ours start getting up at 6:00 A.M.), and you figure that it takes them a little while to fall asleep after getting in bed, you can see that you need to start your bedtime routine at about 7:30 or 8:00 P.M. We usually start at 7:30. It gives us time to tell stories, deal with a trip to the bathroom, make sure teeth are brushed, and still get everyone asleep by 8:00 or 8:30. Even with our son, we kept bedtime at about 9:00 or 9:30 P.M. until he began high school.

When our kids were younger, it seemed that our lives were determined by nap schedules. We were not trying to be perfect parents; the reality was just that if they didn't nap our lives were miserable or at best difficult. Even today, when our kids are older, if they don't get enough sleep the incidence of problems and bad moods goes way up.

Sleeping Is a Priority

Sleep is important—for both parents and children. You need sleep so you're in a positive frame of mind to deal with them, and they need sleep so they can be alert to face the world. An added bonus with early bedtimes is that after your kids go to sleep your house can calm down a bit—I like to think of this as recuperation and replenishment time—and you and your partner have a chance to relax and enjoy some time alone together.

Unfortunately in our culture, sleep is one of the things that people are often willing to sacrifice. We just don't have enough time to get everything done, so we choose to stay up late. Before the light bulb was invented, people got an average of ten hours of sleep a night. Today the average is six hours per night. Unfortunately, it is during the last two hours of sleep that most of the major cell repair, immune-system building, and rejuvenation for your body happen. Dr. Maas says that there are three integral components to your health—nutrition, exercise, and sleep—and of the three, the latest research shows that sleep is the most important.

The qualities you need to promote sleep, according to Dr. Maas, are a regular sleep time; a dark, quiet, well-ventilated room; and a routine. You do not want to amp your kids up on sugar right before bedtime, and kids who are having difficulty sleeping might also forego desserts after dinner. Keep kids away from any caffeinated drinks too—coffee and tea, of course, but also colas, which have the same effect. The routine is your nighttime ritual, which I've discussed in the previous chapter. If you are doing it right, your child will be falling asleep at a reasonable hour, getting in the required amount of sleep, and waking up alert and ready to greet the day with enthusiasm.

CHAPTER 8

GOOD HABITS

At first you are your child's entire universe. Children learn from what you say and, more important, what you do. You are all they have. It is a huge responsibility. I have many friends who could not get their lives together— too much drinking or drugs or partying—whose priorities shifted once their kids were born. Having someone completely depend on you and look up to you gets your attention.

Once you get into a routine with the basics, when you are on kid patrol during the day you find yourself automatically glancing at the clock. As 10:00 A.M. creeps around, you see yourself going to the refrigerator and chopping up carrots or apples or just leaving bottles of water out on the counter. You go into town, or even to a party, and you start assessing how safe the environment is and how much extra attention you have to pay to your child. It gets to inhabit a minor part of your consciousness, but the impact is tremendous.

MAKING A FUNNY SOUND

Going to the next step beyond the basics, you begin to realize that we are our children's first teachers. We take up a lot of space in their lives—literally. We are the ones they look up to. Watch your children as they grow; you will see them mimicking you. It starts with their imitating you as you make funny sounds, like blowing through tightly pursed lips, and continues as they look to you for clues about how to operate in the world.

In the world you set up around your children, you are giving them a tremendous amount of information. Some of it is basic, like taking care of their essential needs and letting them know you are watching over them. Other routines tell them what they need to do to keep their bodies in good shape. A lot of what you show them sets up expectations about how the world does and doesn't work.

SOCIAL BEING BASICS

Brushing your teeth in the morning and evening, bathing regularly, flossing, washing your hands before a meal, using a paper barrier in a public bathroom, covering your mouth when you sneeze, using a handkerchief or tissue to blow your nose, cleaning your fingernails—all these are the rudiments of taking care of your body and being aware of your environment. When you teach your children these things, you are also giving them basic information on how to feel comfortable in society. Watch children whose parents don't pass along these habits, and you often see kids who are not at ease in social situations or who are conspicuous for their not fitting in. It is important to note here that I am not talking about social class issues, like having the latest clothes or being so formal that your child can't be a child. These are just the bottom-line basics of keeping healthy and being comfortable as we interact as social beings.

KINDNESS

At a school we once looked into for our son, they said that the underlying agreement for the whole school was kindness. It impressed me. Whatever they were doing, whether it was a competitive sport or a challenging theatre production, the message given was that you needed to be kind first and foremost and everything else could follow. I grew up in schools where kindness was rare and fighting was the norm at recess from third grade on. Talk about an unsafe atmosphere! I've seen it both ways now—schools where the older kids pick on and make fun of the younger ones, and schools where the older kids play with and include the younger ones. In the former, the older grades are feared and avoided while in the latter the older students are looked up to and admired.

Kindness is a great value to practice in families too. It is challenging. Say you are with your kids on a hot day in the car when the trip starts taking longer than you expected and everyone is whiney and you realize you just missed your exit and are now lost and your three-year-old decides it is time to fall apart—you sometimes have to reach down deep to find any kindness or understanding.

Kindness can be the basic lubricant in a family. It can give everyone the room they need to feel safe enough to move through difficult situations. Instead of reacting and then having to sort out the drama, you end up working together to find solutions.

NICE CROW

As a parent, you also sometimes have to eat crow. After you scream at your kids for not being kind to each other and fussing at each other nonstop all day, it suddenly dawns on you that you are yelling at them for yelling at each other. Maybe not the message you want to be sending.

RANK OUT

I grew up in a community where the culture was the opposite of kindness; in fact, meanness was the norm. Friends would "rank each other out," doing verbal one-upmanship, as a way of playing with each other. You were always looking over your shoulder to see what was coming to get you. As this type of behavior gets to be familiar, you stop noticing how mean it is, and in fact you start expecting it as a sign of inclusion and acceptance. It is a strange way to live, though, and for kids the message is that you better learn to be tough or you won't survive.

KINDNESS WORKS

Fortunately, kindness can get to be familiar too. When your child wants to carry the groceries in for you because she knows your back is hurt, you will realize how much kindness is worth. I remember when my shoulder was injured, my younger daughter would avoid putting her head down on it when she went to sleep at night (one of her favorite positions) just because she didn't want to hurt me. We get back from our kids what we put out to them.

EXTENDING YOURSELF

Extending yourself is a simple manifestation of kindness. It is getting the glass of water—after you have just cooked the meal and gotten up to get the salt and then gotten up again to get the chopsticks your kid suddenly wants. Or it's making a special trip to school with a check for your son's school yearbook; you gave it to him yesterday, but he left it at home in his dirty pants. You don't want to end up being a servant or have your kids expect that they don't have to be responsible for taking care of things. But a million times each day you get to push yourself a little further or do one more thing for your child.

To keep a balance, you also need to ask them to extend themselves for you. At times I have had to remind my kids of all I am doing for them and that it is out of love, but I need them to rise to the occasion too, to clean their rooms, empty out the car after a trip, or just help me clean up the house on the weekend.

PAYING ATTENTION

Paying attention may be one of the most important habits to cultivate with your children. I didn't realize until I was older and had actually learned how to pay attention that my relatives (on both sides of the family, interestingly enough) have pretty short attention spans. They are the sweetest people, but if they ask you a question, they will often interrupt or become distracted halfway through your answer.

I first noticed this when my kids were at a family gathering, responding to questions about what they were doing in school. They were trying to explain the details of a play they were involved in when my aunt, completely innocently, said, "So, dear, tell me about your friends." My kids, who were used to having adults listen to what they said, were completely taken aback. They weren't used to people not caring about what they said. They didn't embarrass my aunt by saying something, but I noticed that later they were less inclined to participate in the conversation.

My wife says family reunions on my side are like a Woody Allen movie. No one can finish a story without someone else interrupting them. It's amusing occasionally, but for children it sends a message that what they have to say is not important. When kids get to be teenagers, they get more secretive and go into their private worlds. If you have been paying attention to them all along, it will be easier to pick up the subtle clues when something is wrong. You will also be letting them know that you care enough to notice.

BE PRESENT

Being present is one of the great spiritual lessons of life, and children can be one of your greatest teachers. People say, "Being present is a present"— it's a gift to be in the moment. Being present means having the flexibility to notice what is going on without letting the past or future impinge on you, and responding with your whole being.

Being present is walking into your son's room to fuss at him for not getting his homework done and for not helping clean the kitchen and for talking on the phone too much, and at that moment hearing him say, "I'm having a hard time with my girlfriend," and realizing that a door has opened and that you can either walk through it, maybe getting into a heartfelt discussion about some real emotions that he is dealing with for the first time, or you can go on with your agenda, getting the kitchen cleaned but losing the moment forever. It happens that quickly.

And without warning. You are just dropping your daughter off early for school, and she says, "Daddy, let's go for a walk," and the practical side of you knows she has time but you do not. Your business head knows you have tons of calls waiting to be made the second you arrive at the office, but somewhere deep inside you know that you haven't gotten any time alone with her for a couple of weeks. So you go for it and get to have your heart open up to a seven-year-old who adores you.

Being present is often inconvenient and impractical and disruptive and time-consuming and exhausting. And very worthwhile.

YOUR WORLD

In the world you give your children, you are also making a world for yourself. If you're kind to your children, they likely will be kind to you. If you pay attention to them, they will usually pay attention to you. And if you are present with them, you will receive the gift.

PART

FOUR

INTERACTING WITH THE
BIG WORLD

CHAPTER 9
SCHOOL

School is more work than you ever imagined it could be. When my first child started preschool I naïvely thought I would put a lot of work in choosing a school, and then my work would be over for a while. I would research the school options. I would go and meet the school personnel. I would take time to get to know other parents who had been at the school. I would explore the philosophical differences in different schools and give a lot of thought to what would be best for my children. I would make my decision and then drop my kid off and go back to my work.

Wrong.

So wrong, in fact, it is a joke. Parents who have kids in school will laugh at this. It starts with meetings—class meetings, all-school meetings, fund-raising meetings, parent-teacher meetings, and special-event meetings. It goes on to class plays and recitals, sports events, holiday programs, auctions, science fairs, class trips, environmental cleanups, and parties. It happens before school, with special classes, and after school, with soccer games or play rehearsal. It goes on in the evenings with lectures and on the weekends with campouts and always somebody's birthday party. Having kids in school is a full-time job.

A FEW QUESTIONS TO CONSIDER

The following issues are ones we wish we had thought of beforehand. They are some of the questions you will confront when your child enters school.

Many children are not ready for preschool at four or even five years old. If you have a choice you might consider part-time preschool. It is important to remember that initially separation is a huge issue for young kids.

Choosing public school, private school or homeschooling is a big decision. Public schools will often offer more diversity and are paid for by your taxes. Private schools demand a lot more parent involvement, are expensive, and can provide a unique curriculum. And homeschooling offers an entirely new approach to learning (see www.naturalchild.org/jan_hunt/unschooling.html).

Before you even arrive at the school, you can choose schools with a special focus (Multilanguage curriculum, arts or science focus) or a particular philosophy or curriculum (Waldorf or Montessori, for example). Some schools excel academically (Blue Ribbon winners for high schools), and some have a religious perspective at the center of their philosophy. You can also speak with school administrators while evaluating a school. Note if they seem to be people you could go to if you had a problem. Other parents whose children attend a school you are considering can also offer you valuable inside information on what works and what doesn't work about a particular school.

On your first visit to a school you can learn a lot. What does the physical environment look like, and does it feel safe? You can view the recess area and make sure it feels protected from the outside world. You'll also notice the atmosphere on a first visit, whether the other kids are playful and seem to be kind, or if competition and aggression are the order of the day. Sitting in on a class can also be quite enlightening. You can see if the children are actively engaged and participating or distracted and bored. The main thing to do is to pay attention to what you see.

The other issue that is always worth researching is how the school handles disciplinary issues. Emergency preparedness (earthquake, flood, fire, hurricane) is probably particular to your area but again is worth asking about. Make sure the school has an active program for emergency response and supplies on hand to deal with any emergency.

PARTICIPATION

Schools are undervalued in our culture at the present time. Look at what teachers make in most areas of the country compared to the salaries of most other professions. In many schools funding has also been severely cut. This means schools do not get maintained, much less improved. It means that special programs—the ones that really add to the school environment, like sports, music, art, and other "special subjects"—either do not exist or are running with very few resources.

The only variable in this equation is you. You get to participate. The one caveat here is that most schools are so desperately in need of help that those who volunteer can quickly become inundated with more and more projects until they burn out. You need to choose what you are up for and what your family can handle. My wife once volunteered to start a school store, and it quickly turned into a forty-plus-hour-per-week non-paying job. We have seen the 80–20 rule played out many times in our school experience: 80 percent of the work is done by 20 percent of the parents. So watch out before you raise your hand or add your name to the sign-up sheet being passed around.

STOP *BEFORE* YOU DROP

If you get involved in your child's school, you will get to know some wonderful, selfless people over the course of a school year, many of whom do much to enhance the school experience. But by the end of the year, you'll notice that everyone has started looking a little dragged out. When it comes to school, it is easy to take on too much, and it is easy to get overwhelmed.

The positive side is, you get to be part of a community. You will work with some incredible folks, and together you can create some truly magical experiences for your children.

BASIC EDUCATION

So you've found a school. Your kids are enrolled. What should they be learning?

Academics begins with "the three Rs—reading, writing, and 'rithmetic." These are essential skills in that so much else is built on these abilities. One of our daughters did not start out as a great math student. She was much more interested in fashion design. It was important to let her know how much math would be involved in doing great design work.

Kids who have a strong grounding in reading, writing, and math are in a much better position to excel in other studies. Look at areas of the world where people are trying to raise the standard of living. One of the first things they put in place is education, and one of the first things to teach is the basics—reading, writing, and arithmetic. Even if you are working in a fast-foods place, you need to know these skills.

In today's world, science and computers are also must-knows. The world is evolving at an amazing pace right now, and both of these studies will give kids the skills they need to be able to operate effectively in the future.

ABILITY TO LEARN

When it comes to educating kids, the saying "Give a person a fish and you feed him for a day; teach a person to fish and you feed him for a lifetime" applies. School will educate your child in the three Rs. But some things you can give them at home.

Support your children's formal education by giving them the ability to learn and an interest in learning. The ability to learn is a daily practice that involves solving problems and encouraging your children to find solutions themselves. Often this means finding the delicate balance between helping them and making sure you're not doing it for them. Whenever you set them up in a task and then step back while they discover the intricacies on their own, you will be fostering their ability to learn. Sometimes you just need to ask your children the right questions to get them started. An interest in learning starts with you being interested in what they are learning. Ask them questions when they come home from school, and then listen. The more engaged you are in their learning process, the more they will begin to see value in their education.

When kids have the ability to learn, they are in good shape. They know where to go to find out information they need or how to begin looking. Coupled with this, if they can think critically, they are way ahead of the game. Children who can discern what rings true, or what is logical given a certain situation, and what makes no sense are way ahead of classmates who can only spew back facts that have been given to them. The ability to learn and to think critically is also the ability to create, which is a tremendous help throughout life.

Kids learn how to discern and think critically by watching you relate to your environment. They'll automatically believe every commercial or movie unless you explain that someone is just trying to sell them something or that a movie is just one person's point of view. If they are taught to check out what they are being told against their own experience, and if they have you to validate their feelings, they have the main tools they need to be able to think critically. When you read the morning paper and tell them that you're skeptical about a politician's photo in front of a day care program because you know that politician just voted to slash funds for public education, you're showing them to not take everything they read at face value. This process hopefully will continue in their school, where teachers will question or challenge them about why they believe a certain way.

YOU NEED TO KNOW

You have found a school you feel good about, your child is getting taught the basics, and you're supporting your kid's education by participating in school activities. So now can you relax? Yes, in that you have set a good foundation for your child's education. No, in that you cannot assume that any school is going to meet all of your child's needs. Maybe your daughter has special needs, like a reading disability. Or perhaps your school is understaffed and does not have the resources to provide extra attention for a subject your son is fascinated with. You need to pay attention and respond.

Situations and Suggestions

- *Situation: Your daughter is having a hard time in math and seems to be going slowly with the basic functions.*

- *Suggestion: Get outside tutoring. Don't wait. Math is a subject, like reading, that is a foundation for other subjects. If students fall behind here, they can get weak in other areas as well.*

- *Situation: Your son loves basketball, but the school has only a mediocre program.*

- *Suggestion: Find a coach in your area who loves basketball and enjoys working with kids, or enlist your partner, yourself, or a friend to coach a city league team, and get your son on that team.*

- *Situation: Your daughter loves guitar, but your school offers only the regular band instruments.*

- *Suggestion: Find a local musician who loves guitar and who can work with kids.*

Schools do many things well, but in some areas they are limited. They are dealing with their own administration, budget crises, curriculum requirements, and disciplinary problems. It is not realistic to suppose that your child will get every need met. This is your child's opportunity to begin to love to learn. And you are the only one who can assess how well this is going.

YOU ASK AND ASK AND ASK

So how can you tell if everything is going right at school? Here are some questions you should pull out regularly and ask yourself:

✤ *Is the school meeting my child's needs?*

✤ *Is my child being seen by his or her teachers as the best person possible? Or getting pigeonholed as a "problem" kid or an "average" student?*

✤ *Is my child adjusting socially there? Am I facilitating play dates after school or on the weekends?*

✤ *Are my kids thriving? Do they wake up most days eager and excited about going to school and what they are going to be learning?*

✤ *Can my children tell me in detail what is going on at school? Or when I ask them do they just say, "Stuff"?*

✤ *Can I connect with my children daily? Are they in their bodies or hyper and difficult to make eye contact with?*

If you do find problems or have concerns that your child is not getting the most out of her or his education, you have to start taking action to remedy the situation. This might mean a phone call or a fax to a teacher to say that you're concerned that Jill has such a poor grasp of basic math functions. You also can request a meeting with a teacher to discuss your child's progress and see if you think the teacher is seeing the best in her.

Our son experienced a rough entry into high school, and for several months we approached a guidance counselor repeatedly, only to get a halfhearted response. Whenever I called the counselor always seemed impatient and distracted. We began to feel like problem parents because of the response we were getting. After four months we decided to go straight to the principal. In one day we got the attention we needed—along with a new guidance counselor. Two suggestions here: always document your concerns in writing, even after a meeting, and make clear requests about what your expectation is ("We want to know what options Austin has for finding a better Spanish teacher").

If you're not getting the response you need from your school, or if you feel your child is not being served by a situation in that school that you cannot change, you may have to consider other schooling options. Most districts will let you transfer to another school, and depending on your work situation, you may be able to consider home schooling for a certain period of time. The only thing you shouldn't do is to leave your child in a situation that is not working. It's a waste of their time, and you're setting them up to not enjoy learning.

You may be the only one who can pay attention and notice when things are not going right and when they are. I have found that when you pay a lot of attention, it makes teachers' jobs a little easier. They know you care enough to notice. And they see you are actively involved in fixing any problems that crop up.

It's a Wild World

School also puts you in touch with the larger community. At school, your

kids get to experience many different cultures and lifestyles. This is great—
and it can also present some challenges for you as a parent. Especially if you
have chosen a school with a strong philosophical basis, you may be tempted
to think that everyone who sends their kids there shares your basic
assumptions and values. If you assume a commonality just because you are
in the same school, you may be in for some rude awakenings.

R-RATED FRIENDS

Our friend's daughter, Anna, came home from another friend's house in first
grade last year and informed her mom that she had just watched the horror
film Carrie. Linda was shocked. She mostly kept her child away from
television and was very protective about any movies she saw, even screening
the G-rated ones to make sure they were sweet and kind. When Linda talked
with the other mom, all she got was, "Oh, I don't think they even knew most
of what was going on." But Linda had to sleep with Anna for the next few
weeks because the little girl was so terrified.

We found out years ago that we needed to tell other parents that we were
very selective about the movies we let our kids see and that anything other
than a G rating was not acceptable. Even then we got surprised. We found
that some families thought mean-spirited movies were okay, which we didn't.
We knew that our younger daughter would get very upset when anyone
was cruel to animals in a movie, so we had to let people know that our
guidelines were pretty strict.

The same is true with food. If your kids have allergies, or if you don't want
them to be eating tons of sugar, you need to let other parents know. Some
parents think that as long as the package says "natural" their children can

have as much of it as they want.

We went on a camp-out once with my daughter's class, and after dinner people brought out supplies for s'mores. We were surprised when some parents put no limits on how many their kids ate, and we watched as kids shoveled down the chocolate and marshmallow sandwiches. Then about 9:00 P.M., when things were starting to quiet down and we were getting the kids ready for bedtime, one of the other parents brought out three quarts of ice cream! Everyone just has different standards, and if you don't let other people know what yours are, you may be in for some surprises. Don't assume a common understanding that may not be there. Truly nice and wonderful people can have completely different rules than you would expect.

CHAPTER 10
TV AND POPULAR CULTURE

A friend of mine who does etchings on stones once inscribed "Kill Your Television" on a stone. I'm not an advocate for the violent destruction of TVs, and in fact we do have a television set, which we use to watch movies, but we stopped being plugged into any channels or networks or cable over fifteen years ago, before our first child was born. At the time it didn't seem like a big deal. It was obvious—why would you want a television in the house when you had children? The picture of coming home to kids who were zoned out in front of the TV and didn't even acknowledge me was not one I wanted to see. Television was not what I wanted to hear, either. Arriving home to a house filled with your kids' voices is quite different from opening the door to the drone of the TV. Even now when I'm working at home, and for any stay-at-home parent, the sounds of children's play and tearing through house makes any TV show pale by comparison. It's a world apart.

THERE IS LIFE AFTER TV

Now, fifteen years later, I can honestly say that aside from a handful of moments (one or two times during the Olympics or an occasional major sporting event), we don't miss the TV. I have worked with people who cannot conceive of this. They say, "Well, how do your kids do in school?" or "Don't you feel like they are missing something?" In answer to the first question, our kids do fine in school. And yes, they are "missing something," most of which, every time I have a chance to watch TV, I get more convinced than ever that they are better off without.

WHAT ARE THEY MISSING?

For one thing, they're missing out on excessive violence. A University of Pennsylvania study showed an average of 20 acts of violence per hour during children's shows. They're also missing out on bad language, overt sexuality (over 14,000 sexual references per year for young viewers), and endless marketing (over 360,000 advertisements by the time they graduate from high school for an average child viewer). Studies have shown that just sitting in front of a screen absorbing images and sound simultaneously hampers children's creativity (Joseph Chilton Pierce, The Magical Child, Penguin USA, 1992).

Peggy O'Mara from Mothering magazine reported in an editorial in December 2002 on research she found in Science magazine (March 29, 2002) documenting an association between television viewing among adolescents and violence. In a study involving 700 young people over a sixteen-year period, O'Mara says, "Of youths who watched less than an hour of TV a day at age 14, just 5.7 percent were involved in aggressive acts by ages 16 to 22, as compared with 22.5 percent of those who watched one to three hours a day and 45.2 percent of males and 12.7 percent of females who watched more than three hours a day. These aggressive acts took the form of threats to injure, general aggressive acts, physical fights, assaults, robberies, and the use of weapons to commit crimes."

IT'S ALL MARKETING

The popular culture is pervasive. And insidious. A mom I know used to watch TV with her kids and announce when each commercial was coming on. The kids did not know the difference between the programming and the advertisements. My daughter, when she watched infomercials, thought they were documentaries. The fact that the entire purpose was to sell something went right by her.

Popular culture is all marketing, and its purpose is to invest you in the brand, whether it is a type of skateboard, a soft drink, or a rock star. It's all about sales. My suggestion is to just wait. Give your kids time to grow up and make their own decisions before they get all merchandised out. A lunch box with a character on it, a T-shirt with a sports company name, or even many of the latest kids' movies are often more marketing attempts than anything else. Your kids can develop their own images, their own sense of fantasy, and their own magic if you just give it enough space to happen.

OUR FAMILY WITHOUT THE CABLE

Although our children don't watch TV, somehow—I think through osmosis—they know everything that is going on in the popular culture. Our kids watch TV for only a week or two a year while they are visiting relatives or friends, but they are still aware of what is happening in the popular culture at any given moment. My son knows jingles to advertisements even though we don't buy the product and don't have TV. And as far as world events go, I guarantee that all of your friends and family will call you the instant anything major happens in the world, as they feel sorry for you and want to make sure that you are included in the most recent catastrophe.

And at our house, instead of watching TV, we play cards with each other or board games, or the kids do art projects or read, or we talk. After dinner we can hear Austin learning a new song on guitar in his room, or I'll sit down to play something at the piano, or Zoë might be practicing violin. Eliana is learning the lines from her school play, walking around the house screaming them at the top of her lungs. Kim might be laying out a project to dye Easter eggs on the kitchen table. Sometimes there are the sounds of kids fussing with each other, or me not being able to find an important letter that I left on the dining room table, or my son making an argument about why he should be able to go see a certain concert in a city twenty minutes away on Saturday night. It isn't always idyllic, but it's always real, and it's always just the sound of our family and not somebody else's story line.

CHAPTER 11
FINANCIAL INTELLIGENCE

You can now learn typing, computer skills, a plethora of sports, theater, choir, journalism, art, and a variety of academics in high school (if your local school hasn't slashed all these programs), but nobody is teaching kids how to balance a checkbook or, for that matter, how to write checks. Financial intelligence doesn't mean you are an accountant or an entrepreneur, it just means you understand how money works. Knowing the difference between credit card interest, which might be 18 percent a year, and a line-of-credit interest, which can be as low as 4.75 percent, can be the difference between making your payments every month or going further into debt. Most kids don't realize how finance charges can affect the final price you pay for your car when you are buying it on time. Knowing how to use a credit card or an ATM is a basic survival skill. Learning what things cost is even more critical. Kids who are brought up having everything paid for have a hard time grasping how many financial decisions are made every single day. Unfortunately, financial education is still not required in any high school and in fact is offered in very few.

For young kids it comes as a shock to realize how many things cost money. They'll ask, "Does it cost money to cook?" You say, "Well, the food costs money, the stove cost money, the gas costs money, the utensils cost money, the pots cost money, and if you eat out you need to pay the people who are working, and to rent the building and for insurance." They start to get the picture.

LEMONADE PROFITS

Opening up a lemonade stand can be a good first lesson in earning money. They'll learn how tricky it can be to make a profit if you ask them to pay you back for the cups and lemonade and napkins. One weekend when Austin was about ten he had a few friends over, and they opened up a lemonade stand at the end of the street. They did a pretty good business and at the end of the day ended up with twenty-six dollars. After he paid for his supplies they were down to twenty dollars, and by the time he split it with his buddies, he had five dollars in his hand. He was a little crestfallen. The following weekend, he went out by himself and started the lemonade stand again. A young friend showed up, and Austin set him up on some pots to bang on. He then added "& Music" to his lemonade sign. For fifty cents you got a cup of lemonade and a song. By the end of the day he had made forty-seven dollars. He gave his young musician friend five dollars, which his friend was thrilled about, paid for the supplies, and was left with over thirty dollars. He learned a valuable lesson about partnerships and marketing that weekend!

FINANCE 101

You don't have to teach them how to read a financial sheet, but it is good to teach them the difference between an asset and a liability. Most kids don't realize that most of the money you put into a car you will never see again. Or that selling your own labor has limited income potential, whereas selling a product has far greater potential to generate revenues. Also they need basic information about how to shop, what a good deal is, or how you negotiate a price when buying a car. Most kids and many adults today are financially illiterate, and yet financial intelligence is one of the most vital skills in being able to operate successfully.

MAKING A LIVING

Through modeling and seeing your kids for who they are, you start giving them some reflection on work they might want to devote their lives to. Finding one's passion is a challenge for all of us, and you can start showing your kids, through your friends and people around you, what their options are. Kids will get very enamored over a certain career, and it is important to explain the risk factors in that occupation and how much income is realistic to receive for that type of work. When kids begin to understand what rent and utilities, owning a car and a cell phone, eating out, insurance, and clothes cost, they can begin to match that up against the careers they're excited about. Understanding the implications of your career decisions can leave kids with a much more realistic expectation of how to achieve their goals. If traveling now is the most important thing to them and they do not want to spend years building a career first, they might get a job in a travel-related field or learn some skills that are easily saleable abroad. Here's where you can also point out friends of yours and show how their careers have created certain limitations in their lives, and how other friends have different opportunities because of the choices they've made. The important piece here is nailing down your information to dollars and cents so kids can begin to get a real understanding of how the world works.

PART

FIVE

HOME AS A
SAFE HARBOR

Chapter 12

HITTING KIDS

Don't.

That really should be the end of this discussion. Whole books have been written on why not to hit your children, but all you need to remember is: don't. If you need reasons:

❖ *You're bigger than they are.*
❖ *It doesn't work.*
❖ *It sends the wrong message.*
❖ *There are always more creative solutions.*

OWN YOUR MISTAKE

Obviously, you are bigger, and if you hit them the message you are sending is that your size makes it okay. Size is an unfair advantage. If you are paying attention, you will feel awful afterward. Looking at yourself, as I have after spanking my son, gives you a terrible feeling. I ended up apologizing in tears.

My son told me that it was okay. I told him it wasn't okay. It's not okay.

If you do blow it, this is my suggestion: Own what you did, be willing to look at your action and understand how you got there, apologize out loud to your child, acknowledge your behavior to your spouse or another adult (having to come clean with another adult about hitting a kid will really put your feelings into perspective), and come up with a real plan for never doing it again.

THE STAKES ARE HIGH

Besides being unfair and a power play on your part, hitting kids also doesn't work. It may stop their behavior, it may give you some temporary reprieve, and it may even bully them into acting a certain way. But you are losing a lot more than you are gaining. You are teaching your child that fear and physical punishment are the reasons to do something rather than love and understanding. You can do this, but you pay a price. The price is love and connection. It is hard for a child to stay open and loving to someone who may slam them if they step out of line.

THE PAIN THAT KEEPS ON GIVING

Physical punishment also sends the wrong message. The message is that this is how we work things out. It tells a child she or he isn't worth much because when a conflict occurs, it will be your way or the child will suffer. This wreaks havoc with kids' self-esteem and gives their self-worth a tremendous bruising. I have known lots of adults who were beaten as kids, and it affected them their entire lives. They were tough, they knew how to survive in the world of hard knocks, but they had a lot of trouble getting close and feeling safe.

THERE'S ALWAYS A BETTER SOLUTION

We're the role models for our kids, for better and for worse, and physical punishment is definitely the worst. It teaches them either to be victims or to become abusers, and neither one provides a model for healthy relationships or a happy life.

BREAKING THE CHAIN

If you were hit as a child, you probably have extra work to do in this area of your life. I have friends who were severely abused who decided in their twenties never to have kids. The idea of continuing the cycle was too frightening to them, and they weren't sure they could change it.

When our kids were young, one grandparent always gave us the same advice. Whenever we would call and say we were having a hard time with one of the kids taking naps or talking back to us, this grandparent would always say, "Well, you might just have to give her a good spanking." We were always sorry we had brought it up. For many people, that is the only solution they know, so you will have to find support elsewhere.

It takes work to break the chain of abuse and physical punishment. You need help, support, and commitment to learn a new way of solving problems. When you do, it will totally change your relationship with your kids for the better. Deciding that it is no longer acceptable to ever hit your children is a courageous and powerful stance.

TIME-OUT (FOR YOU)

Time-outs, when children are sent to their room, are often as much for the parent as they are for the child. Sometimes everyone just needs a little space to calm down and regain perspective. Counting to ten will also work. If it is a choice between hitting a child or screaming at them and leaving the house, leave. Do whatever you need to do to settle down and find a better way to handle things. The important thing is to look at the problem afterward and try to come up with a more creative way to handle it.

ANOTHER WAY

In some Scandinavian countries physical punishment for children is actually against the law. When the law changed in these countries, nationwide poster campaigns alerted people that hitting kids was now illegal. Visitors to these countries a few years after the law went into effect said that initially the law made little difference. People no longer hit their kids, but they did verbally abuse them. It took some years of educating parents on how to deal creatively with problems for things to change. Now generations are growing up who know it is no longer acceptable to hit a child. It sounds like a truly civilized society.

In this country, we still look the other way. The assumption is that disciplining children is a parents' personal responsibility. A number of years ago a song by the group 10,000 Maniacs, about child abuse, included the refrain, "I'm tired of the excuses / everybody uses, / he's your kid, / do as you see fit, / but get this through / that I don't approve / of what you did / to your own flesh and blood." The song is appropriately titled "What's the Matter Here?" (In My Tribe, Elektra/Asylum, 1987). That pretty much says it all.

WHOSE KID?

When my daughter Zoë was about five years old, we walked into a hotel to find a dad just screaming at his little girl, pulling on her hand and forcefully directing her back toward their room. Zoë looked and asked me, "Why is he doing that?" I started to give some sort of "rational" explanation about how he had lost control. Zoë interrupted and said, "Let's go stop him." That was really the only rational response.

JUST SAY NO!

I have a friend who was severely abused as a child who tells me that when she is around someone at a restaurant or in a department store who is being abusive to their child, she kind of blacks out and wakes up to find herself in the other person's face, screaming at this adult to stop hurting the child. Not always the most effective way to handle the situation. And definitely embarrassing and scary when you are there. Yet in a way it seems like this is exactly what our entire culture should do—collectively scream "No!" and help parents find another solution whenever we encounter this type of behavior.

For parents, my strong suggestion is, just don't go down the road of hitting your kids. It doesn't go anywhere you want to go.

CHAPTER 13

BOUNDARIES

Kids are constantly checking boundaries. They want to know where the limits are, to know that the world is safe. Kids need to know how far they can push. Once the boundaries are clear, it usually doesn't seem like a big deal to them. They just want to know what the rules are so they can play the game.

WHAT BOUNDARIES ARE

Think of boundaries as the warning lights, the flashing reminders—"danger up ahead." Many of them will be based on your experience, like knowing that if your kids stay up too late and don't get enough sleep, they will be falling apart the next day. Some boundaries are major, like being careful around sharp knives because you may cut yourself (which may result in a boundary of kids not using a sharp knife until they are a certain age or making sure they use a sharp knife correctly). Other boundaries will be for your comfort, like having your kids check in with you (when they are older) when they get home after being out with friends, even if you've fallen asleep.

Some people think of boundaries as fences or restrictions, but for boundaries to work they should be based on reasonable guidelines. If your children trust that you are interested primarily in their safety, they may not always comply happily with your boundaries, but you will have a much easier time getting them to work. When kids sense that boundaries are arbitrary, not based on anything reasonable and overly confining, they will start to rebel. You can easily avoid many problems by choosing which issues are important enough to set boundaries around.

THE TWO IMMUTABLE RULES

Two rules regarding boundaries can guide you in most situations:

1. *Be kind.*
2. *Be firm.*

The kindness is critical or your kids wills start to confuse hurt feelings or fear with clear boundaries. If you scream at your kids for throwing something at the dinner table, you might get them to stop, but you will be heading toward a disciplinary culture in which the rules are obeyed not out of understanding but out of fear. At the same time, you can't be namby-pamby and soft-spoken or in a sugary sweet voice say, "Now come on, you need to stop that now." This is where firmness comes in. It is important to let kids know what is acceptable and what is not.

CONSEQUENCES

In Indian culture, karma is the law of action and reaction. In John Lennon's song "Instant Karma," he utters the line that could be the watchword for boundaries: "Instant karma's gonna get you." With kids it is important to give them instant feedback on boundary issues. In our home there is an "Eat in the kitchen" rule. Even now that our kids are older, even with our teenager, we still have to police this rule and hold them accountable when we notice it being broken. This might mean immediately getting them to go to the kitchen. And it might mean having them vacuum their room or the living room to clean up the crumbs, which is the reason for the rule in the first place. At mealtime we have clear expectations of the kind of atmosphere we want around the dinner table. We have sent each of our kids at times to their rooms when they were being out of control or picking on each other or using awful manners after being asked not to. In most of these situations, just taking the action and letting them be by themselves for a few minutes is usually enough to turn things around. The guidelines here are:

+ *Kids should know what is expected of them.*
+ *They should know what the consequence will be if they don't meet that expectation.*
+ *The consequence should be appropriate and in proportion to the offense. This is important because if the consequence is totally out of balance with their action, they will sense the injustice and end up remembering the consequence and forgetting why it happened.*

❖ *For example:*

Expectation	Situation	Consequence
House stays clean	Messes everywhere	Plays stops till everything is picked up.
Leave for school on time.	Not ready, last-minute dramas in the morning	Earlier bedtime or no playing until they are ready in the morning.

❖ *For it to be effective, the consequence should occur relatively soon after the boundary has been broken.*

ONE-ON-ONE CONTACT

After you have faced a boundary issue and given your child a consequence, it is always a good idea to meet the child one-on-one to make a connection, talk about what happened, and lead the child back to the rest of the family. Kids often get embarrassed about being singled out or called on something. You need to show them that you are ready to be over it, that they can let go of it and move on to having a good time.

You help them come back, and you let them know that you still love them. It is important that you clearly go over what has occurred. Here are some hints:

❖ *Tell them clearly what happened. Be very specific: "You threw a pea at your sister."*

❖ *Tell them what the rule is: "There is no throwing food at the table."*

❖ *Tell them how it made you feel: "I find it really hard to relax when there is chaos at the dinner table."*

+ Let them know your expectation: "I want to have a nice, calm meal with my family."

+ Remind them, in tone of voice and words, that you are no longer upset and that you still love them: "I love you, now let's go back and have a great dinner."

SHIFTING BOUNDARIES

Boundaries can get very confusing for kids because different people have different standards. It might be you and your partner. Or you and your ex. And there is always the supermom or superdad you end up "competing" with. And don't forget relatives. Once you finally get clear on what your boundaries are, don't be surprised when no one else supports you. You decide that you don't want your kids eating cookies or sweets between meals for snacks. Then they go over to Grandma's, and when you pick them up and notice that the big plate of cookies that was on her kitchen table is gone, she says, "Oh, they just had a few cookies and ice cream. It's okay. They're such sweet kids."

What can you say? I suggest two guidelines here:

+ Get clear on what your boundaries are.

+ Communicate to other people what they are. If your kids are sleeping over at a friend's house, what time do you want them to go to bed? How much sweets do you want them to eat? Are you okay with them sitting in front of the TV the entire time and having that be a "visit" or a "play date"?

You can't control other people, and although you get to state a preference, as the Rolling Stones say, "You can't always get what you want." You need to find the balance between being flexible and knowing what your bottom line is. Eating sweets at Grandma's might be an issue that you want to let go of because the love and tenderness will probably outweigh any health dangers. By contrast, finding out that one of your child's friends' parents has a drinking problem and drove the kids home after school the other day is an unacceptable danger that you will want to draw an absolute boundary on.

Here are some of the areas that become boundary questions:

* *Sleep—When is bedtime? How far can your kids push it before they have to be asleep? Even with babies this tends to be an issue.*

* *Food—Do you cater to their whims, or do they have to at least try what you have prepared? If they don't like it, will you fix something else?*

* *What kind of language is acceptable in your home? How about damn, crap, suck, stupid, ass, and other words?*

* *Can food be eaten anywhere in the house or just the kitchen? How about popcorn during movies?*

* *Hitting—Can your kids hit each other? Or use force of any kind to get what they want?*

* *How many times do you have to ask your kids to do something before they do it—once, three times, no more than ten?*

* *Are you okay with your kids talking back to you? Having a "smart mouth" in front of their friends?*

* *Homework—Do you expect them to do homework or practice instruments on a regular schedule or just whenever? Is it okay if they do homework on the floor*

in the middle of the living room? Do you follow up when they are finished?

✤ *Candy—when or whenever? Can they have their own stash? Is there an acceptable amount or strict guidelines?*

✤ *Boundary changes—Do the same rules apply when they go over to friends' houses or when friends come over to their house?*

✤ *Your neighborhood—Let your kids know the boundaries specific to your area. At what age are they allowed to cross the street by themselves? What are the fire safety rules or the pool rules?*

✤ *Cleaning—Is their room their business or yours? Do they always have to make their beds or only occasionally? Are they expected to put toys away or to help clean the rest of the house?*

Don't React to Your Past

Avoid the loose-parent syndrome. People who were raised with strict guidelines and boundaries may find it easy to flip to lax or nonexistent rules with their own kids. But the problem often wasn't the strict guidelines but rather the lack of love and kindness. Don't burden your kids with your past. Kids can deal with (and actually appreciate) boundaries that are firm, fair, and delivered with kindness.

Clear and Consistent

Kids who are the most well adjusted are those who have been given clear, consistent boundaries. The caveat always is: be flexible—not so much that with a little persuasive arguing you will always relent, but enough so your kids know that you will adapt and make a decision that is appropriate for that moment. It's always a juggling act. Also remember the first truth of boundaries: Kids are always checking them—and sometimes pushing them.

CHAPTER 14

FAMILY MEETINGS

Family meetings give you experience in talking about key family issues—what is going right and wrong and what your expectations are. When holding family meetings, try to keep them:

✤ *Away from the daily routine. In this way you are not trying to discuss a heavy issue while people are digesting dinner.*

✤ *Not crisis oriented. Sometimes you will meet in response to a major issue. But this should not be the only time you have family meetings or everyone will dread them. Also try to balance negative comments with positive ones. If you are talking about how the house is a pit lately and no one seems to be cleaning up, you might also mention how well different children are doing in school or how much you enjoy listening to one child practice violin.*

✤ *Respectful. People have to feel safe and know their opinions will be heard and valued. Being respectful means everyone takes a turn. When someone is talking, two rules apply: (1) everyone listens—meaning their eyes are looking at the other person (this is how you know someone is paying attention—their eyeballs are watching you), and (2) no one interrupts.*

The great thing about family meetings is that they give everyone in the family practice talking and listening to each other. The subtext of a family meeting is:

✤ *We work things out together as a family.*

✤ *Everyone's opinion is respected and valued.*

✤ *We care about each other.*

✤ *We need everyone participating to make this family work.*

You will also be surprised, once you open this door, what your children will bring to a family meeting. Just one suggestion: Don't ever bring up getting rid of any pet at a family meeting (even a neglected mouse or guinea pig); you will be outvoted every time.

You don't have to acquiesce to every demand or request, you just have to listen. You also may encounter many requests or suggestions that need more thought or consideration. The important thing here is not to let things fade into oblivion. At some point in the next week or two, it is important to get everyone back together or at least to get back to that individual and let him or her know your decision.

TALKING SO PEOPLE CAN LISTEN

Communicating clearly means saying things in a way the others can hear you. The idea here is to get away from:

✤ *Blame ("You messed up!")*

✤ *Universal condemnations ("You always hit your sister")*

✤ *Judgments ("Why are you sitting there with that stupid look on your face?")*

Saying, "You really blew it today" or "You always forget about getting your homework done" or "What a dumb thing to do," while it may honestly reflect your feelings, will instantly put up a wall between you and the other person. And it will do nothing to solve the problem.

Many counselors follow a program called the Rosenberg Model (see www.cnvc.org), which suggests four steps to clear communication. Try these during your next family meeting:

1. Be specific. Tell the other person exactly what she or he did. Describe it in detail. For example, you begin, "When you left the kitchen a mess last night ..." But you don't stop here. You describe the mess in detail: "With the dishes all piled in the sink, the floor not swept, and the table with crumbs all over it ..."

2. Say how you felt. Then you tell the person how you felt about it. Not how it made you feel (no one makes you feel anything), just how you felt. For example, "I felt so crummy." Again, don't stop. "I was so exhausted after work, and seeing the kitchen a mess, I felt like you didn't care about it being clean."

3. Say what you need. Let the person know what you need and expect. For example, "I need to feel like we are all helping to keep the kitchen clean and it is not just up to me."

4. Make a request. Ask for what you want. "I want you to clean the kitchen up after dinner." Or "I really want the kitchen to be clean when I get

home from work." Be precise here: "I want the dishes to be done, the table to be cleaned up, and the floor to be swept."

After you have made your request, the other person can respond. The important thing is that you have spoken in a way that makes it possible for the other person to hear you. I have seen this work many times, defusing potentially explosive situations.

LISTENING SO PEOPLE CAN TALK

The other half of family meetings is listening. One way to let people know you are listening is to look at them. This sounds so elementary, but watch people during a conversation. Many times people will look away, become distracted, or start playing with something else, tapping their foot or tearing up pieces of paper. The message this sends is that what the speaker is saying is not important.

My friend Katherine was once married to a man named Mark, and every time they began a heavy conversation he would pick up the remote control for the TV and start clicking through the channels. Not great for a conversation—and lethal for a marriage.

When you are meeting with your kids, you need to remind them to watch the person who is talking and if they start to play with something to put it down and listen.

❖ *Having attention focused on them makes a big difference in what people say.*

Also be very careful when the conversation gets emotional. Then there is even more of an opportunity for people to look away or to try to calm someone down. At these times it is even more important just to keep listening and watching the person who is talking.

BE PREPARED

Regular family meetings are important because you are setting a precedent and getting experience so that when major issues do arise, you will have a structure in place to begin dealing with them. This doesn't mean that you have to hold family meetings every week. Once a month might be plenty for your family, especially if you are checking in with each other over dinner every night and doing activities together on the weekends. The main thing is that meetings happen often enough so that everyone gets some experience going through problems together. If you get to solve some minor problems together, when the big ones arise, you'll have a head start in being able to address them.

CHAPTER 15
SENSE OF HUMOR

When my older daughter Zoë was only a couple of years old, I would chase her around the dining room table. She would be totally determined to outrace me, and I would act totally determined to catch her. Just the sight of her running around the table was so cute that it made my heart do flip-flops and made me laugh so hard that I would double over and have to catch my breath. She would continue to taunt me, running around me and getting closer and closer. At some point I would catch her, and we would both collapse on the floor laughing and laughing. It was pure joy.

THIS LITTLE PIGGY

Keeping a sense of humor in your family melds together lightness, playfulness, and love. Humor should never be mean-spirited or directed at another person. Laugh with each other, even if it's about the silliest thing. The other day we were lying in bed, and one of my girls starting doing "This Little Piggy" on my fingers. Except she was creating long stories about each little piggy: "This little piggy went to market. Well, she just loved to shop. She wasn't the brightest little piggy, but she knew a bargain when she spotted one. Sometimes on the way to the market she would get so consumed by stopping at garage sales looking for the ultimate bargain that she would in fact never make it to market. She would be so sad at these moments until she remembered that there is always more shopping, and up she would pop, off to find another sale." My daughter went on and on. I had no idea where she was pulling it from, but it started getting very dramatic, and my other girl and I were just busting with laughter. Laughter can bring you together.

To promote a healthy sense of humor in your family:

❖ *Never allow humor to be mean or have an edge.*

❖ *Always laugh with each other, never at each other.*

❖ *Don't make a joke out of everything; sometimes kids want to be taken seriously.*

❖ *Let your kids go through their moods instead of trying to make them laugh their way out of it.*

❖ *Try not to take yourself so seriously. Mirroring your actions to each other is a great way to lighten each other up (keep reading).*

❖ *Know when to stop. Especially things like tickling can be oppressive if overdone. Just enough is perfect.*

THE MIRROR

When our kids were younger, we would sometimes all switch identities at dinner. Each of us would take on another personality. I would get to be my son, he would get to be his mom, and so on. It was hilarious to see each of us imitating someone else. Always I was amazed at how perceptive the kids were and how we all had each other down. We would end up laughing at ourselves in the other person's eyes.

Mirroring is also a great technique with kids, especially when they start being teenagers. Within a year or two you go from being the most intelligent being on the planet, someone who truly knows everything, to being a complete dumb cluck. Sometimes when I say something to my son and he gets one of those looks, like, "I can't believe you would even say something so stupid," I will immediately turn around and, imitating him, say, "Dad, you are such a moron, I can't even believe that you can get your teeth brushed in the morning. Jeez, what a dummy," and then I'll keep shaking my head back and forth in disbelief. Usually at some point, he gets what I am doing and just cracks up. Of course, he also explains how he really wasn't saying I was a moron. Right.

PUPPIES

Watch a group of puppies after they start to crawl, and the first thing they do (after nursing) is to play with each other. Play is their most common form of interaction, gnawing and chewing and jumping all over each other. A sense of humor helps us stay playful with each other. It is our common way of just enjoying each other's company. There are always times to be serious and share the bigger things, but a sense of humor is the cartilage between the joints that lets everything move a lot easier.

PART

SIX

KEEPING THE
MAGIC ALIVE

CHAPTER 16

SPECIAL EVENTS

Special events provide a chance to withdraw from the day-to-day routine, a time to slow down and remember what is important. My friend May, when she was doing her nurses' training, did a little informal survey in a nursing home where she was working. She asked all of the old people there—some very wealthy, some of modest means—what they had found most important in their lives. Every one of them, without exception and without hesitation, said, "Family and friends." Special events give us time to pause in our busy lives and reconnect with the stuff that matters.

BIRTHDAYS

The beauty of birthdays is that they are a celebration for each of us, to say how special each of us is.

Our family has adopted Tom Chapin's version of the "Happy Birthday" song (found on the album Moonboat). It's sung to a different tune than the traditional song, but the words are just wonderful:

Happy Birthday, Happy Birthday, We love you.

Happy Birthday and may all your dreams come true.

When you blow out the candles, one light stays aglow.

It's the love light in your eyes, where'er you go.

Birthdays are important. Our friend Marilyn, during a year when she and her husband were both busy beyond belief with work, had put nothing together for their three-year-old Ellen's birthday. That morning Ellen came down the stairs, expecting to see the house decorated or at least some cards sitting on the table, and saw nothing. She just sat on the steps, forlorn. As Marilyn came down the stairs, she heard Ellen saying to herself, "Oh, this little girl is not going to have a birthday this year." Marilyn felt awful and realized she had really blown it. She thought about it all morning at work. At lunch she decided to cancel the rest of her appointments, and she went home and spent a couple of hours transforming the house with streamers, birthday signs, cards, and candles. When Ellen walked in the door that afternoon after daycare, her whole face lit up. Marilyn ran to pick her up, said "Happy Birthday," and they held each other and both started to cry. Before bed that night, Ellen told her mom, "This was the best birthday ever." Good save.

Where we live, in southern California, people sometimes go a little nuts over their kids' birthdays. They rent blow-up structures for kids to jump in, or they hire ponies, magicians, puppet shows, or DJs, or they rent limos and take the kids to theme parks. Birthday traditions can get out of hand. One thing to remember:

❖ *Birthdays are about honoring your child, recognizing how important and special this person is. They don't have to be complicated, and you can choose to celebrate very simply if you want to.*

Some years we just aren't up for a big party with lots of friends, so we opt for a small celebration at home with just our family and a few close friends. Simple parties provide a great balance and let our kids know that having fun does not always mean having a big bash. Small can be special too.

One question to ask yourself when your child's birthday rolls around is, Are we planning a kids' party or a parents' party or a relatives' party or some combination? We've been to many "kids'" birthday parties that were really meant for adults. Be clear when you set it up. If the focus is on kids and playing, make sure you arrange the space for playing. Again, you can keep it real simple. When Ellie was three she wanted a party with just the family—any more people would have been too much for her. When Zoë was four, she wanted a fairy party, which translated into gauze draped over a table outside—very simple yet quite magical.

Some years ago when the kids were younger we hosted a "ball" party. We borrowed tons of balls—everything from small hand-sized balls to giant gymnastic balls. Then we got a lot of helium balloons and tied them onto big strings. We spread the balls out in a large field and then had helium balloons staked to the ground on strings of varying lengths. It was visually gorgeous, and when the kids got there, they immediately knew what to do—play!

Because we live near a coast we are also big fans of beach parties. Our teenager had every single birthday of his at the beach until he was thirteen and wanted a dance party. The beach is perfect because there is always something to do, there is plenty of room, the kids can be as loud as they want, and cleanup is easy. Come to think of it, those are four good guidelines for having a great party:

❖ *Choose an activity (this can be as simple as playing in the water at the beach).*

❖ *Have plenty of room to do it in.*

❖ *Choose a place where kids can be kids (being loud and running around).*

❖ *Make it as easy as possible on yourself so you can enjoy it too!*

Birthdays are also a great time to recall your child's earlier years. You can tell them the story of the day they were born. You can remind them of important events in their life. You can show pictures from when they were younger. A birthday is an important bonding time for you to reflect on all you have done together and how thankful you are to be in each other's lives.

THANKSGIVING

We have a gourmet cook in our home, and so Thanksgiving is always a great celebration. Partly it is a feast, but even more it is a time to be together with friends and family and to really remember how much we have to be thankful for.

Thanksgiving is a great time to invite friends, or other people you know who are single or away from their families, to share the day with you. It's important for a couple of reasons. First of all, it is symbolic of what the holiday is about—to share the abundance and good fortune. Also, a new person adds something new to your dinner and creates a dynamic that can really enhance the experience.

Be sure to include the kids in the Thanksgiving meal. Have them help out with cooking or with making little name tags for each plate or with setting the table or making gifts for some of the guests or gathering flowers to spread around the house. If kids just show up for dinner they do not have the opportunity to really participate and feel a part of the event.

The same holds true for everyone else who is there: try to include them in the preparation. When everyone contributes something, whatever it is, all feel connected in a very real way when you sit down to eat dinner together.

We also use the time after dinner to go for a walk or to play a game that everyone can join in on. It is easy to watch a video, but it really doesn't foster the kinds of connections that are possible.

HOLIDAYS

Besides birthdays, most kids will tell you that their favorite time of the year is around a holiday—Christmas, Chanukah, Easter, Passover, Valentine's Day, and more. Even as adults we carry around memories of these special celebrations from our childhoods. More than just the presents, we enjoyed the food, getting together with family, doing special activities, and having rituals that we as kids came to expect and love.

Start your own family rituals. Choose activities that the kids can participate in and look forward to. Here are some of the rituals we have found that work.

CHRISTMAS AND CHANUKAH

We celebrate both Christmas and Chanukah, having both religions in our family. When the season starts, a few events signal that the holidays are upon us:

❖ *The house fills with the smell of beeswax as my wife starts her yearly candle-making project. She and the kids make enough candles to give away as presents and then light every evening for the entire year for our dinner meal.*

❖ *Almond toffee has become a recent tradition after our friend Marilyn and my wife found an incredible recipe. The toffee is dangerous (willpower flies out the window when toffee is around) and also becomes a part of many presents.*

❖ *We make a gingerbread house every year. I learned the recipe from my friend Caroline, and the kids immediately climbed on board. It happens over a week's time, beginning with a trip to the candy store, which seems to get more out of control every year. When we finally decorate the gingerbread house, two rules go into effect: (1) You can eat all the candy you want, and (2) No fighting. Well, actually, there is a third rule that my wife put into effect a few years ago: (3) I have to put the kids to bed that night. The gingerbread house is also a great event for including some friends. Their eyes get as big as saucers when they see the incredible amount of candy assembled on the table. Last year we made an extra house that we took to a local halfway house for homeless families, which was another great part of sharing the joy of the season.*

❖ *Getting the Christmas tree also has been an annual tradition. We always do it together and spend some time figuring out exactly which tree we want.*

❖ *We light special scented candles for weeks around the holidays. This adds to* the aromas around the house and helps transform the feeling.

❖ Music, special food, special decorations (for the tree and around the house), telling holiday stories or poems, and going to holiday plays or recitals (like The Nutcracker) all make the winter holidays a time to remember. They also help divert attention from the commercial part of it and refocus it on sharing special time together as a family. We try to include a lot of homemade presents in our holiday gift giving: jelly and jam, candles, candy, photos of our family, drawings, and heartfelt notes. The importance here is twofold: (1) the kids can participate in the gift giving, and (2) everyone is reminded that gifts are really just a symbol of how much we love our family and friends.

❖ For Chanukah, a celebration of lights, we read stories about the magic of Chanukah and look forward each night to saying the blessing and lighting the lights. We eat more potato latkes than any human beings should ever consume in any seven-day period. And we play the holiday games (dreidel) and sing the Chanukah songs.

EASTER AND PASSOVER

For both Easter and Passover we focus on a big meal with friends and family and some rituals. For Easter we dye eggs a day or two before the holiday. My wife usually brings out the Ukrainian egg dyeing supplies a few weeks before, so we have a lot of beautifully decorated eggs around the house. Easter morning is always met with full Easter baskets in our home. And we usually do an Easter egg hunt with friends or family sometime before our big dinner. Passover is centered on the holiday dinner, the reading of Passover stories, and the reading of the Haggadah and the Seder ritual. With both of these holidays, our intent is to highlight the holiday stories and some of the tradition, while making our own celebration.

The Tooth Fairy

Besides the minor holidays like Valentine's Day, Mother's Day, and Father's Day, which we celebrate in smaller ways, an important event to recognize is when your kids start losing teeth. This is the first significant life passage that they pay a lot of attention to. The Tooth Fairy in our neighborhood has been known to have a bad memory (or be really busy—we're not sure which) and sometimes has taken two to three weeks to show, but she always comes. She has left notes (written in teensy handwriting), sometimes magic stones, and often some money. Here is another opportunity for you to pinch-hit for the fairy folk and leave some magic in your children's lives. To let you know how special the ritual can be to a child, when we were collecting things to put in the emergency box in case we had to leave our house quickly, my younger daughter added only her favorite stuffed animal and her tooth fairy pillow (with a little pocket to put her tooth in) that her grandma had made for her.

The Traveling Adventure Club

The one thing most kids remember about their school experience is class trips. When our kids were younger, a teacher in town acknowledged this and built a preschool program totally around class trips. They would go on adventures to a bakery, fire station, the ocean, a violin maker, the surf wax factory, a theater, puppet makers—and the list went on. The kids loved it.

You can make your own adventures just by paying attention to what is available in your area: a visit to the eucalyptus trees where butterflies stay every winter; watching the sea lions doze on the beach; a visit to the aquarium; or a hike up to a local waterfall. All are exciting and memorable events for kids.

CHAPTER 17

APPRECIATION CIRCLES

To exit the workaday world and enter sacred space, one of the best ways we have found is an appreciation circle.

Typically we will be sitting around after dinner, and my wife or I or one of our kids will say, "Let's do an appreciation circle." Sometimes if relatives are visiting, they find it a little scary. People often are not used to opening up their hearts in front of each other and are wary of becoming emotional (which of course often happens), so they may make snide comments ("Oh, do we have to?") or try to dismiss it in any way they can ("Let's hear the kids play their instruments"). Unfortunately for them, we are persistent, so we usually push through any resistance. We have seen, over and over, that when people really tell each other how much they mean to each other, relationships deepen and life feels more real. And we all get to remember why we love each other so much.

Initially when we did appreciation circles, we all felt embarrassed too. We just weren't used to it. And when other people put up resistance, we felt like we were putting our friends through some torture and feared that eventually we wouldn't have anyone to invite to our dinner parties. We've seen often, though, that the appreciation circle turns into the highlight of the evening or even the holiday, and friends often comment on how touched they were to hear all the beautiful things that were said.

Many different formats for appreciation circles can work. Sometimes for a birthday, we all go around the table and appreciate the person whose birthday it is. We often don't give any direction to the guests at the table, but by example they see that all they have to do is to look at the person, remember why they love that person, and tell them.

We have also had people appreciate whoever is sitting to their right or left, and this is always an interesting exercise. It is great to have to think about another person and why this person is special to you. In this type of appreciation circle, everyone gets appreciated once.

Last Christmas we tried a new format for an appreciation circle. We were sitting around with my folks, and one of the kids suggested we do an appreciation circle. We wrote each person's name on a piece of paper and put them all into a hat, and each person drew a name. Then we started with the youngest person at the table, and whoever had drawn her name offered appreciation for her. We then went to the next oldest person and worked up all the way to my dad, who at eighty-four was the oldest. It was so touching to hear what everyone had to say. Afterward we all said that circle was the highlight of our Christmas together.

PART

SEVEN

RELATIONSHIPS ARE
THE CENTER

CHAPTER 18

WAKING UP TO PARENTHOOD

In the movie The Family Man, Nicholas Cage plays a successful bachelor who gets a glimpse of how his life might have turned out had he gotten married to his college sweetheart and had a family. One day he is the quintessential single guy living the good life in a luxury apartment in New York, running a high-powered business, and the next day he wakes up next to his wife with the kids jumping all over him to rouse him out of bed.

Having a family is like that—one day you wake up and there are kids' drawings all around your desk at work, pictures of your kids and partner on your desk, and a piano lesson that you have got to get Shelly to at 3:30 P.M. You are scrambling, trying to make sure you have money coming in, your partner has what she or he needs, the health insurance is covered, work around the house is getting done, you are exercising—and life just keeps rolling on. You can get so busy that you almost forget: your relationship with your child and the family is what this is all about.

When my kids were young, a friend, Dave, said, "Spend a lot of time with your kids now; it goes by real fast." He later confessed that he had spent a lot of the time his kids were growing up stoned and felt like he had missed their childhood. Another friend, Marty, who has joint custody of his son but because he lives in a different state and sees him for only a few weeks each year, told me a few months ago, "I feel like I have missed my kid's whole life." My friend Jim told me, "When my kids were young it was inconceivable to me that I could be away from them for even a few days without aching to see them again. Then I split up with Lisa and saw them only on the weekends. A year later Lisa moved up north, and now I see them only on holidays. I feel like I'm missing large chunks of their childhood."

ANOTHER YEAR IS GONE

There are lots of ways to miss your kid's lives. You can get real busy at work or in building a new home, and you miss most of your daughter's fifth year. Some years ago, when I was putting in a lot of hours at work, I realized one day that a year had gone by and I had never gotten to take my kids to school.

Mary Lyn, a writer I know, faced a decision a few years ago regarding a rock-and-roll book she had been asked to edit. The money was big, and she was torn. Her elderly mom had just moved out to live with them, and the extra money could have been used to build a much-needed room on her home for her mom. At the same time, she realized that working on this book was going to take a year out of her life. She kept thinking about her daughter, Ella, and told me, "You know, she's only going to be twelve once, and I'm afraid I'm going to miss it." That stuck with me.

KIDS ADAPT—ONLY TOO WELL

Recently my daughter Eliana, who is just starting to read, excitedly told me she wanted to read a book to me. That evening, though, we ran out of time, and the book just lay open on my bed. A couple of days later she noticed it and this time asked if there was time to read just a chapter, but again I was too busy with work and told her we would try over the weekend. Now the weekend has gone by, and I know that if I don't make time to listen to that book, I'll end up hearing only one page. She'll be fine with whatever time I can give her, but I will have missed an opportunity to hear her sound out the words and share that excitement of discovering a word through sounding it out. Parenting is an ongoing show, but many of the scenes are over if you don't pay attention to them at the time.

❖ *Your kids in some ways will be the least demanding of your time.*

❖ *Kids lower their expectations to match the situation.*

THEY JUST WANT YOU

My friend Alan, who works in the computer industry, after a couple of years of struggling was offered a six-figure position with another firm. There were stock options and an opportunity to make a fortune when the company went public in a couple of years. He even negotiated working at home a few days a week. The bad news was that the company was located a one-hour plane ride away, so when he was gone, he was really gone—not available to help out with the kids or stay connected to them.

Alan started commuting a couple of days a week, and after about two years the strain on his family really started to show. He and his wife were having major fights, since she was mad at him for being gone so much. He would always go through a reentry period with his kids when he came home again. One day, after a serious upset, he said, "You know, this is crazy. The whole reason I am doing this is because of my family, and my family is falling apart because I am doing this." That's the catch-22. You can work really hard for your family, and all they really want is you.

The solution obviously is to find the balance between "the struggle for the legal tender" (thank you, Jackson Browne) and having a life. It's not easy, but it's important to remember that your family is the centerpiece that makes your work make sense.

This is your life. You only have one shot at this, and you have to decide how much of a role you are going to play in it for your children.

CHAPTER 19

DAILY MAINTENANCE FOR YOUR RELATIONSHIP

Before you ever have your first major disaster with your family, I can predict what professional advice you are going to hear. Your daughter may be out of control, talking back to you and telling you she hates her life. Your job may be in shambles. Your son may be really needy and clingy. And the first thing the counselor will say is, "Take care of your relationship first."

THE SUN FOR YOUR FAMILY'S SOLAR SYSTEM

Your relationship with your partner is at the center of your family. Whatever else is going on, if you don't take care of that, you are in trouble. Watch how your kids view you and your partner. You are the sun pouring light into their universe. It's not just their physical needs that you are taking care of but their very sense of safety and place in the world as well. For anyone who has ever had a fight with their mate, the thing that always feels the worst is how much this affects your kids. You can literally see terror in their eyes as the very people that hold their world in place begin to collide and the children's sense of well-being turns to vapor. When your relationship is off balance, one of the first places you'll see it show up is with your kids spinning out of control and acting out. They're trying to tell you something's wrong.

You're First!

In the safety procedures on an airplane, they always say that if you are traveling with a small child and the oxygen mask drops, you need to put your mask on first and then take care of your child. Your first impulse may be to take care of your child, but if you don't take care of yourself, you won't be much good to anyone else. You need to take care of yourself and your primary relationship first.

Your own well should be full, overflowing with water. Then if you go to your partner, and she or he needs a drink, you have plenty. If you go into trying to work on your relationship with no resources—if you feel burdened at work, you are uptight about money, you are run-down and exhausted, and your parents are not in good health—you will have nothing to give. In fact, you will probably resent your partner for needing anything from you. If that happens, it is a good indicator that you are not taking care of yourself. Do that first.

Tune Up Regularly

If you personally are in good shape, here is the next major rule:

+ *Take care of your relationship before it needs being taken care of.*

To keep a relationship healthy, you need to do regular maintenance work. Fortunately, this is a lot more fun than changing the oil on your car. The maintenance work on your relationship is just as critical, though; the relationship cannot run right without it. It can keep going, but it won't be dynamic, healthy, passionate, and alive.

Here is a good relationship maintenance schedule:

❖ *Check in with your partner daily. Check in when you wake up and when you go to sleep. Life happens in the details. "How was your day?" "What did you do?" "I want to tell you what I'm worried about." Does either of you need help with the kids?*

❖ *Be emotionally available. Tell your partner how you are feeling. Reveal yourself. "I'm jealous." "I'm angry." "I'm thrilled." This is what real intimacy is built on. If you are talking yourself out of telling your partner about the real issues, you are in trouble. Start disclosing. Give the other person a chance to be there for you. Take risks.*

❖ *Show Up. Extend Yourself. Be there for your partner when the other needs you. Pay attention. If you are having a party and your partner is working hard to get ready, look around and see what needs to be done. Don't just ask, "Can I help?" That's second best. Best is you noticing the floor needs to be vacuumed and doing it. When you run out of things to do, you can ask, "Is there anything else I can do?"*

❖ *Communicate your love. In thought, words, and action, let your partner know of your love. Every day. It's the little threads that build a rich fabric for a relationship.*

❖ *Appreciate liberally.* Don't take your partner for granted. Give a gift at the holidays. This doesn't have to be an expensive present. Just writing a poem or making a planter box or picking some wildflowers or making chocolate chip cookies sends your appreciation. It says, "I am thinking about you, and I want you to know how important you are to me." Don't save acknowledgements for just birthdays or holidays. Any Tuesday is a fine day for a bouquet of flowers, and any Saturday is wonderful for a walk on the beach.

❖ *Take time alone.* You need to get away with just the two of you, and you need to do it frequently enough so that you can build some kind of a dialogue. We love being with our children, and yet we need time alone, to connect. To have adult conversation. To check in with each other and remember why we fell in love.

❖ *Schedule your time together.* The more complex your family gets and the fuller your lives are, the more you need to schedule your time alone. I used to place a major value on being spontaneous and resisted scheduling time together. I was so wrong. With calendars, we avoid a lot of confusion and last-minute scrambles to get childcare. Now we know when we're going on a walk with each other or taking an evening out or even an afternoon interlude.

❖ *Build something together.* It is great to have projects, besides children, that you are involved in together. It doesn't have to be building a house. It can be planting a garden or picking out some trees for the yard or reading the same book or going to a museum together. You are building memories together, and the richness comes from your common interests and experiences.

❖ *Plan special events.* Have something that you are looking forward to—a vacation, a play that you want to see, a special concert, a holiday event. Things that break up the day-to-day routine and let you enjoy each other's company.

✤ *Dream. Have a vision for what you want to do with your lives. Maybe it is traveling to every national park in the country in an Airstream trailer or visiting every major league baseball stadium in North America. Maybe it is having a bigger kitchen. You know how to shape your days when you have a big dream of something you want to do.*

✤ *Keep your romance alive. You know what works for the two of you. Kissing and hugging. Flowers. Candlelight dinners. Poetry. Walks on the beach. A story that touches you and makes you cry. Whatever you do, keep that spark alive. As you get further into a long-term relationship, this becomes even more important. Romance is the prelude to being lovers, and it's what makes everything else worthwhile.*

THE BOTTOM LINE: RESPECT

The final tool for relationship maintenance is so important that it is in a category all by itself: respect. Honor your partner. See the other person as the best of who she or he is. Give your sweetie the benefit of the doubt. Hold your spouse in the highest regard. In relationships that have been going on for years and are really healthy, you will find people who honor and respect each other. Having another person see you in the best possible way lets you greet each day with a sense of empowerment, like anything is possible. This is what love is all about.

PART

EIGHT

FIXING IT
WHEN IT BREAKS

138

CHAPTER 20

 # WORKING THINGS OUT

A few Halloweens ago, when my son was past trick-or-treating but my daughters were still into it, my son called me with a last-minute change of plans, telling me that he and a friend had decided to go to a party other than the one I had originally agreed to. The new party was being hosted by parents I didn't know, but because I was busy with trying to support my daughters' enchantment with the night, I acquiesced.

The next day I learned from another parent that the atmosphere at the party was a little on the wild side, with drugs and alcohol in wide use. This was something I was definitely not comfortable with. I confronted my son as soon as he got home from school. He readily acknowledged that he was aware there were some drugs and alcohol around, and he said in fact that was one of the reasons he had left early—the whole scene made him uncomfortable.

At that minute I could have continued being upset with myself for letting him go to that party. Instead, I decided to use it as an opening to remind him that if he was ever in a situation where kids he knew were drinking, he was not allowed to drive home with them and that I would always come pick him up. I also told him that if he ever tried drinking or drugs and ended up getting scared, he could always call me and I would come get him, no questions asked. It was an opportunity to remind him that he was growing up, that he would be confronted with many decisions, and that most of all I wanted him to be safe.

You always have to keep in mind where you are going and what you need to do to get there. If your main concern is your children's safety, then even when they end up in a situation that you see as potentially dangerous you have to remind them that you will be available to help them get to a safer place. You are trying to help them make better decisions, but even when they don't you want to remind them that the primary reason behind your upset is that you love them and want them to be safe and protected.

Kids Make Mistakes

Once my men's group was at our retreat center doing some cleanup on the property. We had made the day a father-son event, hoping to spend some time with the kids and to work together. After a while, though, we got caught up in the work and didn't notice when Dennis's son Kyle and his friend wandered off to roam the property.

A day later we got a call from the property owner, and after some minor detective work we realized that Kyle and his friend's seemingly innocent wandering had led them into some major mischief. In the hour they were gone from our sight, they had trashed a parked car while its owner was off hiking on the property. All the windows were smashed, the antenna was bent, and there were major dents in the body—vandalism at its worst. It was a major shock and wake-up call for all of us.

In trying to decide the proper punishment or consequence for Kyle, our men's group engaged in endless discussions. The topic occupied much of our time during that twelve-week cycle. One of the men in our group, a single guy who is also a lawyer, clearly wanted Kyle to have to face the police and pay the penalty for his actions. I remember feeling so frustrated that people were missing a basic truth about kids:

✤ *Kids screw up. They make mistakes. It's a part of growing up*

.

Maybe your kids won't break any car windows. Maybe they won't squirt bleach on neighborhood kids' jackets like my friends and I did one Halloween. It may just be scratches on the side panel of your new car that they absentmindedly put there with a tree branch or chopping down a small tree that you planted while they were trying out their new ax. But it will be something. Sometimes it may be malicious, but often I think it is just kids forgetting the rules and getting caught in the moment. This is not to excuse their action. It is rather to introduce a moment of compassion into confronting the situation so that you can arrive at a solution in which everyone involved can learn.

HOW DO THEY LEARN?

The question we need to ask here has two parts:

✤ *How do kids learn from their mistakes?*

✤ *How do you help them to come to terms with their mistakes?*

You have to invest in your kids and go through this process with them. Investing in your kids is literal. Instead of the quick reprimand or penalty, you have to see this as an opportunity to work with them so they can understand the seriousness of their actions. This takes time. You may need to work with them on buying and replanting the bush to replace the one they chopped down or go with them to talk to the neighbor whose window they broke or just have a serious discussion with them about why they shouldn't fight at school. Labeling your kids as bad or turning them over to the authorities when they're young, while it may shock them into behaving correctly, can also give them a label that they start to be identified with, and it will do nothing to build their relationship with you.

It is important to hold kids accountable for their actions, to have them confront the mistake they made and hear how people were affected by their actions. They can then make appropriate compensation to whomever was involved. Our men's group finally decided that Kyle had to confront the owner of the vehicle and make restitution by arriving at a fair price with her, working to make sure the debt was paid off, and going back to the retreat property to do some real cleanup.

When kids make mistakes it is important to actually connect with them, to break through their walls so they can see how their actions affected other people. You want them to view their mistake as something they did, as a bad choice or an error in judgment, not as something that is integral to them. Since their action involved a choice, it is something they can choose to change in the future.

THE JET-PROPELLED WILDFIRE, ALMOST

One time when my son was about nine, he had a friend over who was a couple of years older, and they were playing outside. I was gone, and my wife had to leave for a few minutes to get some groceries. She had driven a few minutes away from the house when she realized she had forgotten her shopping list. She turned around, and as she approached our house, she saw our son and his friend in the street with a two-gallon can of gasoline, a box of matches, and some toy cars. She stopped the car and screamed at them, *"Stop!"*—at which point both boys looked up at her bewildered, as in, "What's the problem?" A few more minutes and there might have been a huge explosion. In trying to explain later what they were doing, they said they thought they could get the cars to be jet-propelled.

In a situation like this, the easiest thing to do is punish the kids. You're right, they are wrong. But what are they going to get out of it? To learn to be a little sneakier next time? To cause their mischief farther from home? Of course there should be consequences. At the same time, here is an opportunity for you to teach and for them to learn something.

With the gas can incident, they needed to learn how explosive gasoline is and how they could have scarred or even killed themselves. The other part of that lesson was that we live in a high fire danger area, and an explosion could have started a huge wildfire that could have destroyed many homes and also been life threatening. Both were major lessons. That discussion took place over a week after the incident and involved pointing out that car explosions that they had seen in movies were the result of gasoline exploding and that the fireball from two gallons of gasoline would have been huge. We also got information on wildfires and let them see that a wildfire in our canyon with the right winds could cover a distance of a football field in one minute and could literally burn up our entire canyon, and all of the homes and many of the animals in it, in less then twenty minutes. They really were innocent to the consequences when they started their science experiment but afterward realized how serious the implications could have been.

ARE YOU LISTENING TO ME? (NO)

What is definitely not helpful is just to scream at kids and punish them. If you do this, they will not learn anything important, and they will shut down. The last time someone screamed at you, what did you do? You put up a wall. Kids do the same thing, and in that environment, it is very hard if not impossible to communicate.

HONK LOUDLY

Always keep the bigger picture in mind. There is a Zen saying that goes: "When someone is walking in front of your car, it is sometimes necessary to honk loudly to get their attention." It is sometimes important to get your children's attention and let them know that you are upset. Sometimes just your initial reaction—"What are you doing?!"—will get their attention and give you enough time to stop and move on to considering the best way to work this out.

It is also effective and real to let kids see your emotions. When our younger daughter was four years old and we were picking up her sister at school, she got fascinated by what some kids were doing in the playground across the street. Before we knew it, she had darted off across the street without looking. It was only because an observant parent screamed "Stop!" to the mom in the oncoming car, who slammed on her brakes, that an accident was avoided. Afterward, clearly shaken, I held my daughter and told her how much I loved her, that I didn't want her to be hurt, and that it was really important for her to look both ways before crossing the street. My voice was quavering, and my whole body had ripples of emotion going through it. The moment had a big impact on all of us.

YOU CAN BE WRONG

There are also plenty of times when you realize that you are clearly wrong. Maybe the kids did not clean up the living room like they said they were going to, but your hysterical response is completely out of proportion to their actions. Sometimes your mistake is a little one, like not picking them up on time or not being able to fulfill a promise. Whatever your faux pas, be sure to own it and apologize.

One time I was in an argument with my son about a vacation we were going to take that he was not too interested in. To reinforce my argument that my son should go on our vacation with the family and that we should be more important than a camping trip he wanted to go on with his friends, I said, "Well, you wouldn't do that to your other dad (who lives out of state) if you had a vacation when you were supposed to see him." As soon as I'd said it, I realized I was playing dirty pool. He immediately responded, "That's not fair, he lives in a different state and I don't ever get to see him, and I'm with you guys all the time." He was right. I owned my mistake and apologized. It also opened up a great discussion about day-to-day life as compared to being on vacation together, and how they are both important for our family.

My experience is that when you admit you are wrong or own that you are not playing by the rules, you gain a lot of credibility in your kids' eyes. You are also setting up an important model for your children. People can go on forever trying to defend what they did. To be able to admit you were wrong and move on to something else is very freeing. You stop being stuck, and you can walk out of the corner you were backed in. Watching Mom or Dad be adult enough to admit their mistakes instead of wasting time being defensive shows your kids how to do it too.

CHAPTER 21

HARD TIMES / STRESSFUL TIMES

Hard times can put an incredible amount of stress on a family, and they also present big opportunities for a family to grow even closer and more bonded.

During stressful times, like someone losing a job, sickness, a death in the family, or financial strain, many families end up fracturing. You're vulnerable, you have lost your center or that feeling of comfort that the world is a safe place, and you aren't in the best state of mind to be there for your loved ones or even for yourself.

THE SHOEBOX SOLUTION

I once had a major falling-out with a business partner I had worked with for eight years. One of my children was an infant, only seven weeks old, and I was under a tremendous amount of financial pressure. Feelings of betrayal, loss, insecurity, confusion, anger, and revenge all swirled around my head. My family felt the repercussions too and looked to me for reassurance. I had little to give. At the time my wife was incredible. Had she been blaming, unsupportive, or locked into fear, it probably could have pushed me over the edge. Instead, she said, "We're fine. Don't worry, we can live in a shoebox if we need to. I want to be there for you. We'll go through this together." It was exactly what I needed to hear.

Some of the lessons I learned during that time were:

* *Take care of your primary relationship first. This might mean just telling your partner how awful you feel or how scared you are. Let the other person in; do not shut him or her out.*

* *Take care of yourself. You can't get all your care from your partner. Seek outside help. For me this was a men's group. I was also doing peer counseling at the time, and I set up a lot of counseling sessions for myself every week.*

* *Take care of your body. Eat right, sleep enough, get exercise. Don't forget the basics. It is no coincidence that people get sick during tough times—your resistance is down, you are off your regular routines, and you are more vulnerable. Pay special attention to the basics.*

* *Remember to find things that you love to do. Maybe it is swimming or hiking or going on vacation or just reading. These things can give you peace of mind and let you remember who you are.*

* *Have a spiritual life. During hard times you can find comfort in your spiritual connection. This might mean spending time in nature or at your church or reading a book by a holy teacher or meditating, doing service work, or listening to self-help tapes.*

* *Find little successes or accomplishments. Hard times can cause you to lose*

confidence in yourself. Small wins can give your self-esteem a big lift. This can be polishing the car, cleaning up the yard, or getting a small job.

❖ *Look outside yourself. Search the world for evidence that things are all right and life goes on. I remember the spring after my business fallout when the trees started to bud. It reminded me that life goes on, and that was all I needed that day.*

❖ *Do it day by day. It is sometimes clear only in retrospect why hard times happen or what good might come about as a result. You may want to have the cosmic understanding immediately, but often you just have to slog through the tough times—sometimes hour by hour or even minute by minute. This is where a good friend or loved one can help just by being there or saying just the right thing to get you to the next day.*

Rising to the Occasion

Fire tempers steel. I have rarely if ever chosen fire—or hard times in general, for that matter. I usually don't meet hard times willingly. Often I feel upset, angry, and self-pitying, and I kick and scream all the way. But afterward, when the dust has settled, I am able to see some perfection in what has occurred.

I once fought a relationship breaking up for a whole year before I was ready to let it go. It was only afterward, when we were the best of friends and both in new relationships, that I was able to gain some perspective on how well things had worked out.

But even if we don't choose tough times, we always have some power in how we respond to them. It doesn't mean you don't kick and scream or that you're not afraid. Just that in spite of yourself, you rise to the occasion and do your best. Watching you, your kids will learn a powerful lesson on how to meet adversity.

BE THE ADULT

With children, you have to be the adult—even when you feel pathetic and ill equipped to handle what is facing you. Your kids can handle some information on what is going on, but too much is inappropriate. One of my friends tells me that when he was growing up his parents owned an arts school that was always on the brink of financial disaster. For years he lived with uncertainty about what their future was going to be like, feeling that the world was not safe.

Sometimes older kids can be told the simple facts about a situation you are dealing with, but it is irresponsible of you to let them share in your worry. It puts them in a position of having to cope with something that is way beyond their years. Kids are powerless to handle many of the bigger decisions in life. You have to stand in for them and let them know that you are dealing with the situation and that you will get through it.

CHAPTER 22

KIDS ARE RESILIENT

Kids bounce back pretty quickly. This is especially true if you let them process their feelings. Watch your children completely melt down, cry, get angry or frustrated, or be in complete hysterics, and then see how the next moment they let go of it and are ready to have a good time again. It can be a startling revelation. In the moment of the emotion, you are sure you are in for hours of turmoil, and then you blink your eyes and it is over. Some kids may take hours or even days to go through this process. My experience with kids, though, is that once they let go of something, they are done with it. They don't hold grudges and are ready to move on with their lives.

OZ DELAYED

A few weeks ago my daughter and I were spending a delightful Saturday together. Her older sister was away at a friend's, my wife had a catering job, and my son was working on a theater project. Before dinner she asked to watch a movie with me that evening, and I said that sounded fine. We finished dinner and the phone rang. It was my friend Jack, who had just arrived in town. We had not seen each other in years and were scheduled to have lunch together the following day but his plans had changed. Tonight was the only night we could get together. I explained to Eliana and told her that she could meet Jack and hang out with us but I wouldn't be able to watch the movie with her that night.

She first tried reasoning with me, telling me that we had already made plans to watch the movie (true). She then told me how I "never" watched movies alone with her (not true). She finally tried telling me that she was really mad.

I calmly explained that I understood what she was saying—in fact, repeating her words back to her—but that I couldn't watch the movie with her. She then started crying and getting really upset with me. I just let her go through it. About ten minutes later she was fine. She was over it. She asked if she could stay up for awhile with Jack and me, and I said, "I'd love you to," and life went on. The next morning, even before breakfast, we snuggled in each other's arms and watched The Wizard of Oz.

THE TEN-MINUTE RULE

Our friend Sandy, who has been working as a waitress for years, told us about a rule they teach new wait staff:

✤ *Most restaurant crises are over in ten minutes.*

With kids it is often the same. Major hysterics can disappear very quickly. Sometimes just getting your kids fed will completely turn things around. Other times your child might just need a good cry, and all you need to do is listen so they can figure it out themselves or just move on. Some ground rules for a quick recovery:

✤ *Kids need to process their feelings. Your job is to listen and be respectful. Sometimes they need to be held, but do not hold them with the sole purpose of "shutting them up."*

✤ *Remember the basics—have they eaten and slept enough? If not, you may need to cover this before anything major will be resolved.*

✤ *Don't always try to fix it or figure it out. Sometimes kids just need to be emotional. Sometimes there is a solution, and other times you will realize that they just need to go through this. Like adults, kids need to clear away the emotional debris in order to gain clarity.*

✤ *Don't put your judgments on their situation. It is easy to find your own pain restimulated when your kids are hurt, especially if it is a way you were hurt as a child. Maybe you were picked on by a bully (I was). Seeing your child hurt by another kid will be painful, but adding your old hurt to the scene will only confuse the situation. Let them have their own experience without your past adding another level of upset or angst to it.*

✤ *Get over it. Kids process pretty quickly and are ready to move on. If you make a big deal over something or keep asking them "How are you doing?" you will be helping them stay stuck. When they are done, you need to move on too.*

YOU VERSUS THEM

Watching your kids grow up will trigger many memories from your past. It's important to remember at all times that this is their life. All of the baggage of your past hurts, what you wanted to achieve but didn't, or what you have judgments about will most likely be a burden to them if you try to seek resolution through their lives. They need to live their own lives. What they need is your help to find their passion, your support to help develop it, and your wisdom to help navigate through the trials and challenges life throws their way.

KIDS KNOW

Kids can adapt so well to situations that it can be easy to forget that they scar like anyone else. Remember, along with their resiliency there can be deep hurts at the same time.

Watch when kids go through a divorce. They will move into a shared living arrangement and adapt to going back and forth between two households. At the same time, it is obvious that they have been affected deeply. They know on a core level how big of a deal it is that their family has split up. It is no use denying this reality or trying to hurry them through the changes. You just have to accept and acknowledge their process and let them absorb it at their own pace. Your job is to let them know you are available to help.

Even when subtle changes take place in your home, kids can pick up that something is a little off. It is good to let them know as much as they can handle at their age. Most important, be there for them, to talk about what has happened, go to counseling if needed, and remind them that whatever the situation, you are going to hang in there and be there with them through it. That is the most important message you can give them.

NINE

AS YOUR FAMILY
GROWS UP

CHAPTER 23
GROWING UP WITH YOUR KIDS

People who have their children in their early twenties sometimes say that they got to grow up with their kids. I didn't have my first child until I was forty, but my perspective is the same: I'm getting to grow up with my kids.

The reasons you get to grow up with your kids are simple:

- *Kids push you beyond your boundaries and your comfort zone.*

- *You love them enough so that you want to stretch and grow.*

- *Ideally you're still growing and learning your own personal lessons along with them.*

NOT AN OVERNIGHT TRANSFORMATION

I have done this growing only in stages. It is not an overnight transformation. Two things we have found that really support growing along with our kids are:

✤ *A willingness to change.*

✤ *The grace to accept change when it is thrust upon us.*

Once I decided to have kids, everything else followed. The decision had been made, and now I had to deal with the repercussions. No one could have told me beforehand all that this would encompass, and even if they had, it would have made no difference. Before they came into my life, I simply didn't have available the incredible love that I get from my children—love that provides the balance and makes growing up with them worthwhile.

Growing in your ability to be a good parent is a process. By the time my second child was born, I realized that it would be more effective to lie down with her for a nap instead of getting into a power struggle every day, like we had done for months with my son. By the time my third child arrived, I had found better ways of letting her know it was time to clean up her room than just raising my voice. It takes time.

LOSING SLEEP IS DANGEROUS

When my younger daughter was born and we went through that stage of not getting a full night's sleep for days on end, I told myself that I was getting too old for this and it was impossible to keep up with my work with a young baby and we should probably stop having kids. And then I went on to the next day. That, in reality, is all you can do. It is impossible to wake up three times with your baby one night and then have enough brain cells left to get an important letter out to a client the next day. All you can do is to get through that day and pray for some uninterrupted sleep the following night. You do it day by day.

MAKE YOUR KIDS A PRIORITY

The people I have seen who have the best relationships with their kids, and seem to be having the most fun, have one thing in common. They have made their kids a priority. They get to experience life with them. This really is what parenting is about—getting to see the world through their eyes.

In Carole King's song "Child of Mine," (Writer, Epic, 1970) she says, "Although you see the world different than me, sometimes I can touch upon the wonders that you see." Your kids can provide the window to innocence once again.

In Steve Conn's song "Eliana," about a newborn (you can hear a sample of it at www.steveconn.com), he says:

No one has told her that love won't last,

Or that dreams don't ever come true,

No one has told her that people are strange,

If they don't look just like you.

Eliana, lend me your eyes,

Let me see what you see,

Oh, Eliana, Oh, Eliana.

The ability to see the world through your children's eyes is constantly available to you. The key is just to listen, go for a walk together, draw a picture together, or just talk. It is a continuous glimpse into the magic.

In this process you also get to grow up in two big ways.

1. You get to see a part of your own childhood that you may have forgotten or never had the chance to experience.

2. You get to grow as an adult and really learn patience, responsibility, commitment, boundaries, sacrifice, compassion, and love at a much deeper level than you ever have before.

Watching Yourself

Some people say that the stages in our lives are cyclical and that as we get older we repeat things we experienced while we were younger. With kids, you see parallels between your own life and your children's, and things they are facing may mirror issues you are confronting.

When my son was thirteen I went to a parenting workshop and learned about a parallel cycle between children who are thirteen to sixteen years old and adults who are in their early fifties. This was identified as a time of going out into the world and deciding what you are going to do with your life. My son, Austin, at this time was just entering high school, a much bigger pond than he had ever played in, and was getting a chance to see who he really was and what he wanted to pursue. At the same time, I was reevaluating a twenty-year history in the natural products industry and thinking about what I was going to contribute to the world. I was able to offer a deeper level of support to him when I saw how similar were the decisions we were both facing.

If we are all here to learn from one another, it would make sense that some of our struggles would have points in common. With your kids, you can also find genetic traits at work. You see one of your kids being melancholic or moody or having a hard time losing, and it dawns on you that you are really the same way. You get to be more compassionate with what your child is going through and also use the information to help yourself grow.

Observe yourself in social situations with your kids, especially ones in which you are uncomfortable. It could be going to school and meeting new parents and kids. Family gatherings with relatives are also prime times for getting your buttons pushed. You can watch your child acting awkwardly and encourage them to play with the other kids more while at the same time realizing that you are just as uncomfortable but you just know how to hide your emotions better.

FIGURING IT OUT, TOGETHER

Kids are often great reflectors of what is going on, just because they are not as sophisticated as adults in shaping their disguises and masks. Take children to an adult party, and they will often cling to you and not want to go anywhere. I'm usually just as uncomfortable, trying to make conversation or connect with people, but I've wrapped my discomfort in polite chitchat or getting something to eat or standing on the edge of a conversation with a drink in my hand but not really participating.

When I've seen this, it has been a great opportunity to realize:

❖ *How uncomfortable I am.*

❖ *That many other people at the party are probably just as uncomfortable.*

❖ *I can take a chance and push through my unease, reach out, and try to engage someone in a conversation.*

Growing up with your kids also takes down the division between you. It lets you remember that you don't have all the answers and that you are figuring out this world in the same way that your children are. You can help each other grow through it.

CHAPTER 24

SOLID BASE

As you journey down this road with your children it is important to keep in mind that you are moving them toward confidence and competence— confidence in themselves and their ability to meet the challenges they will face and competence in their ability to surmount those obstacles. Having a solid base means that kids are equipped with the tools they need to venture out and meet the world on their own terms.

Kids grow up. In the middle of their youth it seems like it goes on forever. But having watched a number of kids become adults now, I know it definitely happens. In the same way that there is nothing you can do to speed it up, there is also nothing you can do to slow the process down. Time accelerates as they get older. Where the age of two might seem like it takes years to get through, by the time they are teenagers, a year seems to go by in a couple of months. This is all to say that you should begin building their solid base now.

THE MOVE TOWARD INDEPENDENCE

Our job as parents is to give our children a solid base, a real foundation so that they can transition to life on their own at some point and be successful. We are their teachers in showing them how the world works. We are also their teachers in preparing them for that eventual day of departure.

The process of your children leaving comes in steps. School is a big jumping-off point to evaluate how well you are doing in preparing them for the outside world. Sleepovers, vacations, trips to spend time with Grandma, and even just a meal at a restaurant are all check-in points to see how strong a foundation you are giving them.

IT'S THE SIMPLE STUFF

Listen to Sidney Poitier's life story, (The Measure of A Man, Harper Collins, 2000) and you get a clear idea of how important strong family values are. He was raised on a tiny island, named Cat Island, in the Bahamas, and his family was dirt poor. They had no running water, no indoor plumbing, and few possessions. His mom would gather large stones and sit in front of their house every day with a small hammer, pounding them smaller and smaller and smaller until they turned into gravel, which she would then sell. At the heart of their family, though, lay the core values of self-esteem, self-worth, honesty, integrity, hard work, and determination. These values held them together and led Sidney Poitier to become an international celebrity. These character-building values cost nothing, and yet they are worth everything.

CHECK IT OFF

By going through your life with your kids, and following the guidelines I've outlined, you are probably covering the essentials for your child to successfully enter the world. Just to make sure, you may want to review the Solid Base Checklist in the appendix.

CHAPTER 25

CHANGES

Change happens. It's about the only constant in the universe. In our home it seems to be evenly divided between things breaking down—a crack in the ceiling that goes unfixed for years, the yard needing major cleanup, messes everywhere, the portable phone that stopped working last week, and occasional meltdowns with the kids—and things building up: the kids growing and learning new things and developing their talents as musicians, unending drawings and craft projects, making planter boxes for the garden, canning peaches and plums and apricots, continual deepening of our relationships.

IN RETROSPECT

Many of the changes families go through are apparent only after the fact. In the midst of them we are too busy with life to notice. Relatives or friends who have not seen your family for a while will remark how much the kids have changed, and it is then that you stop and realize, "I guess so." When my daughter was two years old, my wife took a picture of her in a dress on the stone walkway behind our home. A week or so later when I uncovered the photo on the kitchen table, I had to catch my breath and shed a few tears. I realized that my baby was growing up; she was now a little girl. I needed to step back enough to notice.

MARKERS

The classic marker on a kitchen wall where you measure your kid's height is a great way to watch the changes over the years. When your kids get to be teenagers and you see them growing a couple of inches in a few months, you will start to think that if you listened carefully, you could hear their bones creaking as they transform so quickly. Kids too like to see how much they have grown from year to year.

Planting a tree or any shrub that you are going to have for a long time is a wonderful way to watch time slipping by. We have three Christmas trees in our backyard that were all about two feet high in a little pot when we planted them, and now they tower over the house.

Photographs and videos also provide great markers for viewing changes and watching your family grow. Sometimes when friends or relatives visit who haven't seen us in a while, we will pull out old albums to search for photos of when we were together years before. When looking at photos, always try to tell your kids the story contained in the picture—what you were doing, how you felt, and what that moment was like. It will allow the photo to come alive for them.

Probably the best way to view and communicate changes is through an oral tradition of constantly telling your family story to your partner and your kids. This happens in pieces, when something happens to trigger an old memory. Passing by the basketball hoop after you've just dumped the garbage might trigger your memory of when your son was three years old, still toddling around with a droopy diaper hanging from his butt and shooting his little nerf ball at the basket you had put up on his crib. Or picking up your daughter and feeling how big she's grown might make you remember when she would sit perfectly still in one of your hands and you could easily raise her above your head. It's important to share those memories with your partner and your child when you see them. You are passing along your family's story to them and your knowledge of it is a sacred trust. Kids love hearing these stories, and hearing them will enhance all the other pieces of their past that you have shared with them. It's a great reminder for you about how long you've been with each other and an important reminder for them about how much they have grown up.

KIDS CHANGE FASTER

Kids are always changing, and often we need to catch up with them. Some of these changes are dramatic, like the day my son stepped off a plane after being gone for a few weeks and his voice had changed. Others are more subtle, like someone wanting a later bedtime because they are older or needing a new style of clothing or just noticing you in a different way ("Dad, your breath really smells in the morning") when they were oblivious before. For parents it is important to recognize the changes and adapt. It's also important to acknowledge the changes in your thoughts and actions.

When my older daughter turned eight she was moving toward being more grown up. She kept pushing for her own room, which we just couldn't do. My wife suggested we get her a bunk bed, saying Zoë had mentioned them.

I kept thinking it wasn't an exciting enough birthday present, but I finally acquiesced. When I saw Zoë's face light up on her birthday morning, I knew we had done the right thing. She took the top bunk, and that became her own world. She absolutely loved having a place that was her own separate area. When we first set it up for her we made sure that her younger sister knew that it was Zoë's private space, and we also gave Zoë her own night light so she could stay up a little later and read after Eliana had gone to bed. For Zoë the move was huge—the exact recognition she was looking for that she was now a bigger girl.

AND WANT YOU TO STAY THE SAME

I said before, kids like stability. When my sister was in fourth grade, my mom decided to change her hair color. She came home with a blond streak in her brunette hair, and my sister just burst into tears. I have been thinking of shaving off my mustache for a while, but every time I mention it my kids get upset. They want me the way they have always known me. I'm not saying parents aren't allowed to change. Just realize that the change will have a big effect on your kids, and you might want to prepare them beforehand. For me it might mean that I have them there with me when I shave and they get to participate in the process. We have found that if we let our kids know what is coming, and they have time to incorporate it into their lives, they do much better with the change.

HELPING KIDS DEAL WITH CHANGE

Sometimes even when kids know change is coming it's tough for them. Losing a favorite pet or having a friend move away makes big changes in their lives that you need to acknowledge. You might not be able to do anything about it other than be with them through the experience. That in itself is a big lesson. Part of being a family is that we can be there with each other through these transitions.

A couple of years ago a German student, Kajetan, came to live with us for a year. It was an incredible experience, and during that year he became part of our family. He was the older brother my son never had, a constant playmate for our daughters, and an older son for my wife and me. When it came time for him to leave, it was devastating for everyone. We were all in tears. The lessons here were important, though—that you sometimes have to say good-bye to people you love, that it's painful to say good-bye, and that our family had really grown. Before Kajetan left we made sure the kids had time to connect with him and tell him how much they loved him. And we all cried and held each other. We also told them that Kajetan would always be in our lives, and in fact we immediately started making plans to visit him in Europe in a few years.

HAVING A VOICE IN CHANGE

Kids need to know that change is just part of growing up, and they need to know that their voices are being heard.

Sometimes, though, there are times to say no to change—that you don't agree with what is happening in your town or your world—and in those moments as well it is critical to teach your children that their voice is valued and important. Maybe their school has a new policy that they don't agree with. Show them how to start a petition, or ask to speak at a teachers' meeting, or write a letter. All of these skills will give your children confidence that they are not powerless, and they will learn what actions they can take when they disagree with changes that affect them.

Keeping the Center

The values you've given them, like being in touch with their feelings, their connection with you and their friends, and their own self-esteem, will help them keep their center in the midst of change. All of these things allow them to experience the change fully in a healthy way and then move forward.

CHAPTER 26

RITES OF PASSAGE

The change happens in the blink of an eye, but it's not a butterfly coming out of its cocoon. One day your daughter is playing with Playmobil™, and the next day she is on the phone for hours chatting with her friend about a certain boy. But a day later she may be back to playing with her dollhouse, so if you're not paying attention you may miss the transition. Then one day you will see your daughter get dressed up for a dance, and you realize a major shift has taken place.

Rites of passage are ways to honor this time of transition at adolescence. While some rituals are about young people "becoming men" or "becoming women," many kids are not ready for this. It's scary for them to think about becoming an adult, and in many ways they still want to be kids. Think about rites of passage as placing a bookmark in time—for you as much as for them. You are getting to pay attention to what an amazing shift is taking place in their lives.

Right now our older daughter is getting ready to go to cotillion next year.

This is very low-key in our town (it's a class taught in a room that serves as an aikido studio during the day), but it is still a big deal to her. She will be learning how to dance and entering into a different social relationship with boys. She has been talking about it a lot, asking how you choose who to dance with, figuring out how to make money for a new dress, and letting us know that we cannot stay around there on her first night. Our challenge is to support her with enough interest to let her know we see how important this is to her, and at the same time not make such a big deal out of it that it overwhelms her.

Rites of passage can be honored in many ways. Most likely you will use a variety of these. Along with some of the more formal rituals, you can begin acknowledging this time by redoing their rooms (repainting or just moving the furniture is a good start) or with some new clothes. Religious rites of passage may include a reading from the holy scrolls (bar or bat mitzvah) or a formal joining of the church by the young person. Spiritual rites of passage may be a vision quest where the young person goes into the wilderness by himself or herself for a couple of days or hikes up one of the mountains in Yosemite.

For Austin we found a ten-day wilderness canoe trip outside of Toronto that he got to experience with a group of other adolescents. This also included a plane flight across country, the first one in which he was not met at the other end by someone he knew. A friend of ours held a weekend retreat for her daughter, Lily, gathering together all Lily's friends and their moms. They had all known Lily for years, and everyone brought old photos from when she was growing up. Lily's mom had blown up some baby pictures and other photos of Lily that were placed all around the barn where the retreat was held. Over the weekend everyone told stories of Lily and all of the times they had shared together. A group of men we know in Idaho found a cave that you could enter only by climbing down a rope through a hole in the ground. They lowered the boys down one by one, then the men descended, built a fire, and they all sat around for hours telling stories about growing up. In any rite-of-passage ritual what you are looking for is something out of the ordinary, an event outside of regular time, which can make this a special moment.

For teenagers the rites of passage will be transmitted by the culture if you don't start the dialogue on your own. Drinking, drugs, smoking, and of course sex are all some of the more obvious ways teenagers can announce their growing up. My suggestion is for you to initiate these discussions before the culture does. I found a teenage recovery group that came to our school and shared their stories about drinking and drugs with my son's sixth-grade class. The stories were heartfelt and powerful and made an impact on all of us regarding what these substances can do to your life. For smoking, the American Lung Association came and gave an incredible presentation that included letting the kids see and feel a healthy lung and a tar-filled lung. With sex, I decided that there was a big opportunity for Austin and me to cross an important line together—which led us to the sex talk.

THE SEX TALK

After I decided I needed to have the sex talk, though, I put off doing much about it. I watched the months go by and had to admit how scary and uncomfortable this was for me. It is uncomfortable for most dads, and parents in general, which is why they avoid it or don't do it or hope the school will take care of it or assume their kids know what they need to—

or will learn it from friends—or throw their kids a book to fulfill their parental responsibility.

I'd Rather Not

Finally a few weeks before my son's thirteenth birthday, I announced to him that we were going to have our sex talk. Big surprise, he tried to do the same thing I had done as a teenager—slough it off with "No, I don't want to." Unfortunately for him, I was more persistent and committed than my dad had been. Then he tried reason: "But I read the book already." I felt my resistance wane. The knot in my stomach cinched tighter, and my breaths grew shorter. At this moment the easiest thing in the world would have been to acquiesce. I only pushed through because I have made a commitment to face things I don't want to face in my life. This one was a glaring sign flashing neon, and I knew I had to follow it.

Cartoon Sex 101

The book my son said he had read is the one we chose as our guide—it was the only one we had. It was comprehensive, presented the material in a straightforward manner, starting with the meaning of the words, and used cartoons for graphic illustrations. The cartoons were safe—a perfect entry point. Yet they were explicit enough to give him all the information he needed. The book also made sure that we wouldn't leave anything out.

Sex Takes Time

The thoroughness was both good and bad. Good in reminding me how many issues were involved. Bad in realizing this was going to take much longer than I had thought. Hopefully you've laid the groundwork over the years with your child by giving your child a basic understanding of the human body and a level of comfort regarding their body.

We ended up spending six one- to two-hour sessions on our sex talk. The talks weren't just about making love or masturbating. We needed to cover birth control, relationships, babies, responsibility, abortion, and even anatomy. Also part of what we were doing was just getting comfortable talking about the subject. This takes time. My son needed to hear me say "penis," "vagina," "breasts," "sexual intercourse," and some common words about sex a number of times before we both got over our embarrassment. So the time is actually part of the message. We had to go through it. It is a dialogue.

It's the Discussion, Stupid

The discussion was as important as the information. We would always do our sessions lying down on our backs, side by side. I didn't answer the phone or let anything else distract us. Lying together was perfect, kind of like we were cuddling, and it was a nice way to approach this subject. He didn't feel like I was staring at him. He was able to have his own reactions. I think sitting at a table would have been too much like a lecture and we would have lost a lot of the connection we were gaining. We were doing something together rather than me just telling him something.

The Questions

I found that the honesty of our setting opened the door for me to be able to ask him some intimate questions I had never broached before, like, "Are you feeling pressure from your friends to be sexual?" "Have you tried putting on a condom?" I let him know that he was going to have these experiences and I wanted him to have the right information. I also let him know that he could tell me or choose to have it be private the first time he masturbated and that this was a rite of passage too. If he wanted to I would want to honor him in some way, or he could just keep it to himself— it was his choice.

BECOMING VULNERABLE

In going through the sex talk with my son I shared my own experiences when I was thirteen—how I fumbled, mistakes I made, how I really didn't know but had to pretend I knew, and what I learned. We both learned to talk about sex, and our relationship grew in a big way. It wasn't just about sex, it was about both of us revealing what we didn't know. We were becoming vulnerable with each other. It was so scary that often my chest would tighten and my heart race as I tried to settle in. And then at some point, it would shift and we would both just be there, hanging out, two guys talking about the real stuff in life. We had crossed an important threshold. My son realized that now everything was open for discussion and I was willing to relate to him on a different level. The shock of it took some getting used to—for each of us. We were wearing new clothes and needed to get comfortable in them.

I SEE YOU

Rites of passage make an important declaration. You are announcing to your son or daughter, and maybe to their friends, relatives, church, or temple, "I see you." You are declaring to them that you see who they are, that you see them growing up and that you are recognizing their moves toward independence. The fact that you see them in this light is huge. That you are willing to relate to your child on a new and different level is an important demarcation in their walk toward maturity. You can also choose to begin revealing yourself to them on a more adult level. The sex talk is a wonderful opportunity to share with your teenager some of what you went through when you were growing up and what you learned. Sharing on this level can open a new era in your relationship with your child. You are in fact reestablishing the eldership and passing along some basic information, as people have done for centuries, about a few things you have found that work in this life.

CHAPTER 27

TEENAGEDOM

Angie and Ralph, friends of mine in Washington, got together when Angie's daughter Naomi was seven. By the time Naomi turned twelve, they were thinking of having another child. Then Naomi's teenagedom hit. By the next year they had completely changed their minds on a new baby. They decided that going through the teenage years with one child was enough.

The teenage years are an explosive time:

* *Bodies change.*

* *The peer group becomes intensely important.*

* *Boundaries are tested almost daily.*

* *The import of school and grades becomes more serious.*

* *Kids move into their sexuality.*

* *Hormones rage.*

✤ *Kids have opportunities to become much more devoted to their passions and talents, like sports or music or art.*

✤ *The reality of a career starts dawning on them.*

✤ *The separation from parents and family starts in a real way.*

DRUGS ROUND OUT THE EDGES

It is no surprise that twelve, thirteen, and fourteen are prime ages for kids to begin experimenting with drugs, alcohol, and smoking. Eighty-five percent of the people who smoke began when they were fourteen years old. With all that is going on in teenagers' lives, reality can be a little harsh and drugs take the edge off (or at least round them out a bit). Watch when people smoke—before classes, during an intense meeting, after sex. These are times when uncomfortable feelings come up, and it is easier just to hit the "off" button, or at least the dimmer switch. Alcohol and drugs are of course the same thing—ways to numb out a bit and make life a little easier to deal with. They also come at a big price, affecting health and emotional and intellectual development. They can also move from being a hobby to a major preoccupation, which is when things get dangerous.

PROMOTE DISTRACTIONS

Last year we heard a master teacher lecturing on the teenage years, and she said:

✤ *If your kids can just find something to distract them for a few years, from about twelve through sixteen, they will be fine.*

The distraction can be guitar, writing, theater, sports, singing, art, a specific subject in school, sailing, skiing, mountain-bike riding, or hiking. It can be almost anything that can consume them, fire their passion, and keep them so engaged that it is the first thing they think about when they wake up in the morning. If they are eager to do it after school or on the weekends, even better. Ideally it should be something that:

❖ *Lets them grow as human beings*

❖ *Develops their talents*

❖ *Challenges them enough to keep them interested, and*

❖ *Helps them express more of who they are.*

WHAT TEENAGE BOUNDARIES?

Teenagers develop the belief about the time they turn fourteen or enter high school that all boundaries have magically dissolved. Some of the questions you may face:

❖ *What is the problem with me staying out late?*

❖ *Why do I have to be home by 12:00 or 1:00 A.M., what's the difference?*

❖ *Why can't I go out with my friends on weeknights?*

❖ *Why do I need to do my homework when I get home from school?*

❖ *Why should I start my report now? It's not due for two months.*

❖ *What's wrong with these clothes?*

✤ *Why do you think I'm lying?*

✤ *Why do you want to know where I'm going?*

✤ *Why is it important to have a parent home for a party?*

✤ *Why do you have to talk to their parents before I go to their house?*

✤ *Why do I have to spend the weekend with my family?*

✤ *Why would I want to go on vacation with my family?*

✤ *Why do you ask so many questions?*

The degree to which they can keep you isolated from other parents is the degree to which you can be fooled into thinking that you are the only parents with strict boundaries and considerations.

When our son entered high school, all of the above questions came at us rapid-fire. This was compounded by the fact that within the first three months of school, he started going out with a young woman who was a senior. He also joined the theater program, and his social life took a dramatic upswing. He was invited to parties every weekend. This took us all by surprise. We weren't sure what the rules were, and we scrambled to find what was appropriate for our fourteen-year-old son. At the same time, we wanted to support his new social scene, to the degree to which we felt comfortable. We learned in the process that many of the parents, even of juniors and seniors, shared our same concerns (drugs, drinking and driving, safety) and that we were not imposing unreasonable limits on our son's social life.

Where Are You?

The first boundary that we set was *accountability*. We wanted to know where our teenager was. The new high school he was attending was an open campus. This meant that he could leave for lunch. We were willing to go along with this, but we wanted to know when he was leaving the campus and where he was going.

This quickly evolved into our rules for parties. We again wanted to know where he was going and when he was going to be home. (We set an upper limit of 12:00 midnight, which was a big change from the year before, but because he was hanging out with seniors, and because some events were not over until 11:30 P.M. and then they wanted to go to someone's house to hang out, any earlier was not realistic.) He needed to tell us the name of the family, and their address and phone number. We also wanted to know that an adult was going to be home. Our son chafed at these requirements, but he did agree to them—mostly because we followed up and made this a stipulation before we agreed to him going out. I should also note here that normally we would not have been so willing to support our ninth-grader entering into this type of social scene. It happened that we really liked the group he was in, the parents were attentive, concerned, and involved, the kids were motivated, creative, and had good standards, and we felt relatively safe.

Following Up

Teenagedom happens fast. So many things are changing, and you get hit with decisions at the time you least expect to. You can have rules in place, but you are not always in the best position to remember everything you should be checking up on.

The rule of thumb here is: follow up. Let your kids know that if you expect something of them, you are going to follow up and make sure it has happened.

No Rational Thinking at 11:30 P.M.

One night our son called up at 11:30 P.M. and asked if he could spend the night at a friend's house. A group of them had been on the beach at a bonfire, and one of the girls invited everyone to stay over at her house. In our town this is not unusual. Teenagers, boys and girls, will all sleep over at one house after a dance or party, with everyone putting down sleeping bags in one big room and falling asleep at some ridiculous hour.

What made this decision hard was that (1) I was asleep and couldn't think straight, and (2) I didn't know the girl whose house he wanted to sleep at.

I told him that I preferred to be asked about sleepovers earlier in the evening but was willing to agree, if he would call me with the girl's address, her phone number, and the parents' names as soon as he arrived there. I then went back to sleep.

My wife woke up a couple of hours later and yelled to me that our son was not home. I assured her that he had called and it was okay. I awoke in the morning and realized that he had never called me. An hour later the phone rang. It was my son, who quickly explained, "We were just so tired when we got there we just fell asleep and I forgot to call." I told him how his mom had worried and explained why it is important that he call. He apologized and told me he would be home in a couple of hours.

More Is Revealed

That evening we had some friends over for dinner, and in the course of the conversation, something my son said led me to realize that he definitely had not "just fallen asleep" when he got to the girl's house the night before. Later when we were alone, I confronted him. He was caught and admitted that he had just forgotten to call and again apologized.

And More

The next day my wife was talking to the parents of another girl our son had invited to the party with him. We had been supervising this girl earlier the evening before, prior to their going to the bonfire, and had assured the parents that she was okay. In talking to this girl's parents, we learned that no adults had been present for the sleepover the night before.

Now What's the Truth?

Again I went back to my son and confronted him. We eventually worked it out and put some new expectations and agreements in place about sleepovers.

The point here is that the follow-up is continual. You keep getting new information, and you have to care enough not to let it just slide by, even if you have already dealt with a related issue three times.

Truth or Peers? Duh!

For teenagers, in the race between doing something with their friends and telling the truth, the friends will always win. It is not like teenagers don't want to tell the truth, it's just that when it seems to interfere with their social life, the truth seems kind of expendable.

The dance here is being able to be flexible and give them enough room for them to do what they want, within your limits and expectations, if they continue to be honest with you. You can't sacrifice the truth for their comfort or else you will be in a rudderless ship. This takes paying a lot of attention and having the commitment to confront them when you realize things don't match up.

One of the first times I caught my son lying was when he was running off to a friend's one evening and I asked him if he had fed his dog. He immediately said yes in an assertive and assured tone. It didn't make sense that he had found the time to do it, but I started to talk myself into believing him. Then I suddenly remembered that I had checked earlier in the day and we were completely out of dog food. I confronted my son, and he admitted he had lied. We talked about it, and he told me how stupid he felt as soon as the words came out of his mouth but how he had got caught up in it. I told him that it was important for him to be honest with me, or I would have to start questioning everything he said. I then let it drop.

Later that evening, in thinking about it, I recalled two other times during the prior weeks when I had questioned him about something he was doing. I suddenly realized that those were also lies. The next day I again confronted my son and he told me that he had indeed lied on the other occasions. As these were all still "first" lies, we spent a lot of time talking about the truth and how it gave relationships and families a strong foundation.

Sex

After the sex talks I shared with my son, we were confronted with some big questions about sex. One day when our son and his girlfriend were in his room and the door was closed, I knocked and realized it was locked. When I called his name he said, "What?" in an annoyed kind of tone. The subtext was, "You're bothering me." I stood there, uncomfortable and not sure what to do, but I said I didn't want him to lock the door when they were in the room together. He opened the door, and his girlfriend was lying on the bed, under the covers. Very casually she smiled and said, "Oh, hi." Both of them had their clothes on, but I immediately realized my wife and I needed to get clearer about what the boundaries were regarding sex. Some of the boundaries we set and the issues we discussed with our son with regard to sex:

❖ *No locking the door when he is in the room alone with his girlfriend.*

❖ *No sex in our home when his younger sisters are home.*

❖ *We weren't sure how we would feel if his younger sisters weren't home, but we would cross that bridge when we came to it.*

❖ *If they were moving in a sexual direction, they first had to go to Planned Parenthood or a family planning center and make some decisions about birth control.*

❖ *A sexual relationship was much more involved and had a higher level of responsibility attached to it, both physical and emotional.*

It should also be stated that our responses to this situation have been very contextual. That is, we really liked our son's first serious girlfriend, trusted her, and felt that their relationship was evolving at a healthy pace. Had this not been the case, we probably would have responded differently. In talking to our son about the guidelines we set up, we also were clear about these not being written in stone and that they depended on the relationship he was in.

It's Not Your Stage

With teenagers, it's important to remember not to set the stage for them. You're there to help, not take over. It's not your time, it's theirs. They have to find their own way, even if it means struggling against you. For this process to work, you need to own your role as a parent. This might mean setting boundaries about what time they are expected home and then holding them accountable or giving them a consequence when they are not. It could mean staying in touch with their schoolwork, like knowing what they are reading in their English class. You might pull a story off the Internet about something they are preparing a debate on, but they have to do the work. And often it means just waiting for that moment when your teenager wants to talk, being there to listen, and maybe offering a few words of advice. Be aware that the time line is often theirs, not yours. All you can do is provide the opportunity, the openness, and the trust to allow it to happen.

And Remember Your Sense of Humor

Especially when your kids are teenagers, try to keep a sense of humor. There is a lot of drama at this time in kids' lives. The changes are so intense, and they stack up so quickly, that they can be overwhelming. You are also often in the position of being the "bad guy" or "the enforcer." You are the one making sure the rules are being followed and the schoolwork is being done and checking in to be in touch with them. It is a thankless job, and one easily met with resistance. Having a sense of humor at times can remind teenagers that they can still be playful and that there is a light side to every cloud. It also can keep you from going crazy and getting too caught up in your kids' dramas.

OTHER PEOPLE

The best thing about teenagedom—and what makes everything else worthwhile—is that at some point, in a much deeper way than you have ever experienced, you start to see your children as just other people. You can begin relating to them and playing with them and working with them as adults. To have this deep bond and at the same time see them as completely separate beings is amazing to experience. You slip back and forth between remembering them as babies and seeing them go off on their own. At first it is hard to believe that your little guy is starting to have girlfriends and be sexual. And then you are sitting across from him at the dinner table laughing and realizing how much you totally adore this person and how incredible it is that you have gotten to grow up together.

PART

TEN

WHY ARE YOU DOING THIS ?

CHAPTER 28

BEING THE BEST MOM AND DAD

Today a friend died. After September 11, 2001, I wrote, "The one thing that is clear is that all we really have is each other." Today that is more apparent than ever. In 1980 I almost died from an infection that went systemic. I lay in a coma for three weeks. During that time I realized clearly how thin the thread is that connects us to this life. I understood the illusion of solidity and saw that the firmness with which I imagined I was rooted to this life was gone. In a second I was cut free and drifting far away from all those I loved and all that I held dear. It took a supreme act of will and some incredible medical help to come back into this body. Maybe the strongest pull on me was my kids, who I was still ten years away from having. Some part of me knew that I was supposed to come back here for them. Our kids and families tie us to this world in the most real way. They also are a constant reminder of how precious this life is.

YOU CAN DO ANYTHING

Having a parent or a teacher or a mate who sees you as the best person you can be is one of the greatest gifts in this lifetime. When someone has faith in you and believes in you, it gives you a tremendous source of support and inspiration, and you can achieve all that you set out to achieve. Your children also see you in your best light, with their innocence intact; they believe you can do anything.

Many people who have been unable to quit drinking or smoking or doing drugs or begin taking themselves seriously will suddenly leave their bad habits behind after their children are born. You know you have someone completely dependent on you and that you're pretty worthless if you're under the influence or numbed out. But the other motivator is having someone believe in you so completely that you actually get to rise to the occasion.

IT'S ALL POSSIBLE

Your children and family are one of the best opportunities in your life to be the best mom or dad or even just the best person you can be. All those things that seemed impossible before come within your reach when that intense love and bond are at the center. You really can be the best mom or dad starting today. It doesn't take money or position or assets. It just takes a lot of love, the right intention, and total commitment. You don't even have to do your best. You just have to try to do your best. You will be amazed at how much is possible when your only goal is to love your child as much as you possibly can.

CHAPTER 29

YOUR CONNECTION

What it all comes down to, in the end, is your connection with your family.

I feel like I've known my wife and kids for centuries. Not necessarily in other lifetimes, maybe just as souls or particles of light that finally got a chance to become human. And even if our becoming a family was the most random of occurrences, the value we place on it and the intention with which we hold each other have elevated our relationship to another level.

We have been given this one lifetime to be with each other, and each moment should be cherished. Out of eons, we get to share this one lifetime in each other's arms. It is a gift beyond all others.

At times I realize how quickly it could be gone, and in fact is going by, and I want to make sure to treasure each moment.

Each one of these people—my children and my wife—I would have walked to the ends of the earth to find. I would have gone on miraculous quests, slain dragons to locate them—and yet here we are as a family, and we get to be with each other. It seems so simple and so spectacular at the same time.

Sometimes I sit here and say, "I get to live with these people," and am stunned. What did I do to deserve this? What contest in heaven did I win that these souls chose me to incarnate with? And then at other times it is obvious and organic. We belong together.

We are each other's connections into something much more profound and greater than our individual lives. Each of us holds a piece to this mystery, and we get to see it unveiled together.

It's not a question of keeping this perspective at every moment but rather a choice of using this perspective to come back to center. There are days when my wife is on me about not helping get the house cleaned for our dinner guests, which I really don't have time to do because I've been trying all day to get a piece of work done, or I've found out my teenager is getting a lower grade on his progress report because of homework that wasn't done after I let him go out both nights on the weekend with the understanding that his schoolwork was done, or just that the house is a mess and nobody seems to be helping clean it up, that I forget what a privilege it is to go through life with these four people. Some days the chaos feels more like the Simpsons than like creative disarray. These are the people I love the most, and they're the ones who can also drive me the most crazy. They push all my toughest buttons, and I can easily be my worst as well as my best self with them.

At times like these, remembering the privilege of loving them and feeling our connection is a choice I make. It's what can open up my heart and bring me back to all that I hold dear. Even on days like these—and sometimes especially on days like these—there is a reason we're together. We get to go through the good times and the tough times together. I choose to hold their care as a sacred trust that has been given to me. It's not always easy, but it's always worth it and it always helps this life make sense.

How we choose to be in this world with our family members will affect their lives every single day. Why are we doing this? It's because it connects us to something far greater than ourselves and in the simplest and most profound way is our single strongest act to make this world a better place. It's a gift both to ourselves and to the future.

NOTES

Schoenthaler, Stephen. "Institutional Nutritional Policies and Criminal Behavior." Nutrition Today 20(3), 1985, pp. 25–39.

Schoenthaler, Stephen. "Diet and Crime: An Empirical Examination of the Value of Nutrition in the Control and Treatment of Incarcerated Juvenile Offenders." International Journal of Biosocial Research 4(1), 1983, pp. 25–39.

Schoenthaler, Stephen. "Types of Offenses Which Can Be Reduced in an Institutional Setting Using Nutritional Intervention: A Preliminary Empirical Evaluation." International Journal of Biosocial Research 4(2), 1983, pp. 74–84.

Schoenthaler, Stephen. "The Los Angeles Probation Department Diet Behavior Program: An Empirical Evaluation of Six Institutions." International Journal of Biosocial Research 5(2), 1983, p. 88.

Schoenthaler, Stephen. "The Northern California Diet-Behavior Program: An Empirical Examination of 3,000 Incarcerated Juveniles in Stanislaus County Juvenile Hall." International Journal of Biosocial Research 5(2), 1983, pp. 99–106.

'Open wide the door to morning', from 'Seven Times The Sun' by Shea Darian (Gilead Press, 1999) used with the permission of the author.

'Hook', Screenplay by P.J. Hogan and Michael Goldenberg, Columbia – Tri Star Pictures, 1991.

Appendix: Solid Base Checklist

Many bricks go into building a solid foundation for kids. Some essential ones are:

* *Honesty*—with yourself and other people. Kids who are brought up learning the value of honesty will actually try lying at some point just to see if you are paying attention. Place a high value on honesty, and explain to your kids why.

* *Spirituality*—a belief in something other than themselves. Our kids attend a nondenominational Sunday school that gives them a grounding in all of the religions. It also gives them the basic moral tools: honesty, trust, compassion, kindness, service, and more. Your spiritual connection may be the ocean or a redwood forest. That's fine, as long as you can introduce your kids to the sacred.

* *Operating Instructions*—For getting around in the world. If you are in an airport, where do you go to get a ticket, and how do you find out which plane to get on? What do you do if you get lost? Where is it safe and where is it not safe? How do you take care of basic needs—eating or going to the bathroom? If you go out to eat, how do you handle yourself in a restaurant? Or if you go to a theater or a concert, what is proper behavior? With this information, kids can operate with some degree of confidence in the world.

* *Safety*—Where to walk in the city and where not to. How to get help, starting with calling 911. Basic defense skills like aikido or Model

Mugging or kick-boxing or running away and screaming loudly. What they need to pay attention to in the current social climate, like date rape or rophies, the "date rape" drug. And, most of all, how to avoid dangerous situations.

✤ *Social Graces*—Shaking hands with someone when you are introduced to them, looking people in the eye when you speak with them, thanking people for having you over to dinner or a party, asking a guest if they would like something to drink, introducing your friend to someone they don't know, excusing yourself when you leave the table, basic table manners. All the simple social rules for how to fit in.

✤ *Respect*—For themselves and their elders. How to show common courtesy to people older than they are. A high value placed on respect also tells them that they deserve to be treated well.

✤ *Communication*—Can you let people know what you want or need? Can you listen to them to get the information you are trying to get? You can practice this daily with your kids in almost everything they do.

✤ *Health and Hygiene*—What they need to be healthy: good food, protein, lots of water, a minimum of sweets and carbohydrates, adequate sleep and exercise. What they need in social graces: using a tissue to blow your nose, washing your hands before a meal or after going to the bathroom, brushing your teeth before bed, and taking a shower or bath.

✤ *Service*—How to contribute to a better world. Whether it is cooking a meal once a month at a halfway house or helping someone in need build a home, doing a cleanup project at the local beach or giving a stuffed animal to a Christmas drive for needy kids. Helping people out is an essential lesson for understanding what's important in life.

* *Working Things Out*—Even young kids need conflict resolution skills— one of the most important tools in life. There will always be conflict, but do your kids know how to problem-solve? Do they know how to find a solution? Can they suggest a compromise in which everyone might win?

* *Making a Living*—Helping kids find their passion through modeling and through seeing your kids for who they are. You can start showing your kids, through your friends and people around you, what their options are.

* *Financial Intelligence*—Knowing how to write a check or use an ATM. Learning how many things cost money. Basic information about how to shop, what a good deal is, or how you negotiate a price when buying a car.

* *Academics*—Beginning with the three Rs—reading, writing, and 'rithmetic. Kids who have a strong grounding in reading, writing, and math are in a much better position to excel in other studies. In today's world, kids also need to know science and computers.

* *Ability to Learn*—Kids who can find information and can think critically are way ahead of the game. The ability to learn and to think critically is also the ability to create, which is a big help throughout life.

* *Sex*—It starts with kids wanting to know where babies come from and can get as in-depth as you are comfortable with. Children need to know what their body boundaries are. They also need to know what is

appropriate behavior with other kids. As they get older, they should have an understanding of basic anatomy, how babies are born, birth control, STI's, responsibility, abortion, and emotional intimacy.

✤ *Emotional Health*—Being there for your kids when they get upset lets them start having a healthy emotional life. Being able to know what you are feeling is first—many adults don't. Being able to express your feelings is next, whether it is anger, love, happiness, frustration, or sadness. Kids don't have to go to therapy to be emotionally healthy; they just have to be listened to and given enough space and respect to experience their emotions.

✤ *Self–Esteem and Self–Respect*—Every child who is held in high regard and who is treated respectfully can have self-esteem and self-respect. These are two of the most essential qualities to be able to succeed in this world and to have a good life. It cannot be overestimated how important these qualities are.

✤ *Music and Art*—Besides being a universal language and a doorway in to deeper truth about the world, both music and art will keep your child's heart open and help to nourish the spirit.

Think of these essentials as a toolbox that you are assembling for your child. Your kids are going on a quest, on an adventure into a magical land, and you want to make sure they have everything they need to reach their goal. You will impart these skills over their childhood and young adulthood, and the important ones will have a huge impact on their lives and many others around them.

INDEX

sugar and sweets, 53, 54, 98–100, 118–119

Here's What Parenting Experts Are Saying About "How To Be the Best Lover: A Guide For Teenage Boys"

"This book is not only a gift to every teenage boy on the planet, it is also a gift to their parents and to every person they will love."

Dawna Markova, Ph.D.,
author of How Your Child Is Smart and Random Acts of Kindness

"What a wise, straightforward, funny and necessary book! May millions, male and female, read it."

Ina May Gaskin,
midwife and author of Ina May's Guide To Childbirth

"Bravo! Finally a book to lead our young men into the world of sexuality with their hearts wide open. We are now impatiently waiting for the second book - A Guide For Teenage Girls!"

Michel Odent,
author of The Scientification of Love and Birth Reborn

"Women's well-being begins when we claim what truly gives us pleasure. This book helps to make that possible within a loving, committed partnership. It advocates an open heart and deep honesty as the path to sexual pleasure - which naturally moves young adults toward wise decisions and away from reckless behavior. Powerful."

Jennifer Louden,
author of The Woman's Comfort Book
and creator of Comfortqueen.com

"Who before has ever dared to tell teenage boys
the deep truth about lovemaking?

Thank you, Howard Schiffer! Your courage breaks down
stereotypes and provides real information that inspires
individuals, strengthens relationships and protects families."

Peggy O'Mara, Editor and Publisher, *Mothering*

How to Be the **Best Lover**
A Guide for Teenage Boys

Howard B. Schiffer

How to Be The Best Lover – A Guide for Teenage Boys is a
road map to lead our young men into the world of
sexuality; What they need to know about relationships, the
responsibilities that come with intimacy, the rules for getting
close and most importantly knowing *when* you are ready
for this territory.

www.heartfullovingpress.com or
www.howtobethebestlover.com

The Companion Book for
"How to Be the Best Lover
A Guide for Teenage Boys"

First Love
Remembrances

Howard B. Schiffer

This is the "other half of the conversation", what you always wanted to know ~ how it really was for teenagers the first time they had sex, the first time they made love, and their first romances. Stories from people around the world!

www.heartfullovingpress.com or
www.firstloveremembrances.com

Easy Order Form

Fax orders: (805) 687 3042
E-Mail orders: orders@heartfullovingpress.com
Postal orders: Heartful Loving Press, PO Box 30041, Santa Barbara, CA 93130, USA
On Line orders: www.heartfullovingpress.com

Please send me more information on:
__ Other books ___ Speaking / Seminars ___ Mailing Lists ___ Consulting

Name: _____
Address: _____
City: _____ State:_____ Zip: _____
Telephone: (__)_____ E-Mail Address: _____

Book Orders

Please send me the following books.
I understand that I may return any of them for a full refund if I am not satisfied.

How To Be A Family – The Operating Manual $19.95 x ___ = $_____
How To Be The Best Lover – A Guide For Teenage Boys $19.95 x ___ = $_____
First Love / Remembrances $29.95 x ___ = $_____

Sales tax: Please add 7.75% ($1.55 per book) for
orders shipped to California addresses. $_____

Shipping & Handling:

U.S. $4. for the first book and $2. for each additional book.
International: $9. for the first book and $5 for each additional book. $_____

Total: $_____

Payment (please circle one): CHECK / CREDIT CARD: VISA, MASTERCARD, AMEX

Card Number: _____ Exp. Date: ____ / ___
Name on card: _____
Signature: _____